HARRY ENFIELD

AND

HIS

HUMOROUS

CHUMS

PENGUIN BOOKS

Published by the Penguin Group under licence from Lyons Partnership, L.P.
Penguin Books Ltd, 27 Wrights Lane, London W8 5TZ, England
Penguin Putnam Inc., 375 Hudson Street, New York, New York 10014, USA
Penguin Books Australia Ltd, Ringwood, Victoria, Australia
Penguin Books Canada Ltd, 10 Alcorn Avenue, Toronto, Ontario, Canada M4V 3B2
Penguin Books (NZ) Ltd, 182–190 Wairau Road, Auckland 10, New Zealand

Penguin Books Ltd, Registered Offices: Harmondsworth, Middlesex, England

Published in Penguin Books 1997
10 9 8 7 6 5 4 3 2 1

Copyright © Harry Enfield, 1997

Scripts from *Harry Enfield's Television Programme*, series one and two, and
Harry Enfield and his Chums, series one and two, reproduced by kind permission of the BBC

Filmset in Helvetica

Made and printed in Great Britain by Butler & Tanner Ltd, Frome and London

contents

'I'd rather be dead in a field than have tea with the Enfields.'

Virginia Woolf

'Harry Enfield,
lauded by his equals, feared by his rivals
and loathed by all and sundry.'

Peter Cook

HARRY ENFIELD

AND
HIS
HUMOROUS
CHUMS

About ten years ago I appeared on *Wogan* as myself. The next day a man came up to me in the street and said, 'You're Harry Enfield, aren't you? I *love* your characters! Stavros cracks me up and as for Loadsamoney – he's the biz! But I saw you on *Wogan* last night – you're a right prat in real life, aren't you?'

Being the sort of person who hates disagreeing with anyone, I said, 'Hmm, yes I am. Sorry.'

'Don't worry about it, Aich!' he continued. 'It's nice to meet you anyway! Be lucky!' He shook my hand and sauntered away.

I'm a 'character' comedian, best known as the people I play, least known as myself. This is my personal inside story of how a 'right prat' transforms himself into other 'right prats'.

I never wanted to be a comedian – it just sort of happened. My ambitions as a child were pretty standard for a boy. At three I wanted to be a cow, at five a train-driver, at seven a fighter pilot, at ten a footballer, at thirteen a pop star, at fifteen anything but a virgin, at seventeen anything please, please, please but a virgin and at twenty I didn't have a clue. Six months later, I was a comedian and I still am.

Before 1982, when I co-wrote and performed my first comedy show, I'd been on stage five times in my twenty-one years of life. My first performance was as a Roman soldier in the school nativity play. I don't think I was a very convincing guardian of the Roman Empire as I was fat and four and in the second performance I wet my pants and burst into tears, so the next year I was demoted to being a bunny rabbit. I next appeared on stage aged ten, to collect the form prize (I was a terrific swot, with round National Health glasses and everything). Then, aged twelve, I was in my prep school play *The Thwarting of Baron Bolligrew* in which I played Obadiah Bobblenob, the egg-painter. It wasn't a huge part, but I decided to do it as an impression of Frank Spencer, and in the weeks of rehearsal I became more and more mad and gave myself lots of extra lines and squeals and odd noises. When it finally came to the performances, the parents watched in silence until this demented looney appeared and wailed and jumped up and down until they all laughed. I remember not getting off the stage when I should have done, carrying on wailing offstage in the middle of other boys' lines – in short, ruining the play for all the other performers, but having a great time myself. Afterwards, I remember my dad beaming with delight. On his way out after the performance, he'd overheard one of the other parents saying, 'I think it's marvellous that they gave a part to that mentally deficient boy, and the other boys were so patient with him.' Dad thought this was brilliant.

My first performance was as a Roman soldier in the school nativity play. I don't think I was a very convincing guardian of the Roman Empire as I was fat and four and in the second performance I wet my pants and burst into tears, so the next year I was demoted to being a bunny rabbit

I Never Wanted to be a Comedian – It Just Sort of Happened

JULIO GEORDIO

With so many South American footballers going to the North-east, it seemed natural to exploit Paul's brilliant vocal dexterity with the creation of Julio Geordio. Julio would be equally at home on *The Fast Show* – he is simply a topical version of Paul's 'Channel 9' presenter ('*... etho per concurra Boutras Boutras Ghali deminacos son terra Chris Waddle ...*') or his Rowley Birkin ('... eewe ethhe hem wrep neffe huge roar Grrr! hensen meef 'fraid I was vey drunk at the time'). We wrote Julio Geordio about ten months before he appeared on screen and were terrified that *Fantasy Football* would come up with a similar character before us, but luckily they didn't.

Tony
Julio Geordio, five games for Newcastle and five goals. Superb performance. Will you be celebrating later?

Julio
Coucourerra eh metha fassa touto conca gannin' oot th' neet wi' th' lads like meta caltho.

Tony
Right ...

Julio
Pete catho potchouli a quandro reet good swalla tito pe mesto anato corla tor dethdo Twinkles night club des ta danca thetherro itho coco athera donco get absolutely arseholed.

Tony
You're fitting in well with your team mates, then?

Julio
E merco lactaroth netza coto got myself a BMW Convertible agaros on buerto to muerto sio me dunto quattro tasteless mock Georgian Hoose catho potchouli a quandro high jinks in the hotel wi' the lads beta duo bato shagged that Danny Beer like.

Tony
Julio Geordio, footballer, gentleman, stud. Barry.

(Julio does arm sex movement.)

Julio
Denthero athta ola! Ola! Ola! Gagging for it.

Tony
Barry.

When selecting my 'first team' for *Harry Enfield's Television Programme,* I was looking for a mix of the young and old, the rich and the poor. The poorest of the poor were the Slobs. The inspiration for Wayne and Waynetta came from the council estate I used to live on in Hackney, East London. It was a run-down 1930s estate, full of rubbish and covered in graffiti, and most on the council waiting list would not consider living there – hence their policy of letting out some of the flats to ex-students like myself. The rest of the estate consisted of a mixture of single mums who did the best they could – when you entered their flats they were always havens of cleanliness and order – and nutters, ancient skinheads with Rottweilers, Old tattoo-covered women wandering the estate in search of a fight and other hopeless cases. There were also a few families who just couldn't get it together to get themselves moved off the estate. Below my flat was one such family. A big fat mum of about thirty, a tough-looking dad of the same age and five filthy but beautiful children aged between three and fifteen. The seven of them lived in a tiny three-bedroom flat meant for a maximum of five, but overcrowding didn't seem to be one of their chief concerns – for Christmas one year they gave the three-year-old a pair of German shepherd puppies. Also, of course, the telly was permanently on at full volume. Despite all this, they were a surprisingly happy bunch. The children would spend their days mucking about on the potholed asphalt four floors below their flat. They were skilled at opening locked car doors, although being well-brought-up children, took care not to damage the vehicles they played in. I often used to approach my own car to see the door flung open and all the children pouring themselves out on to the ground, leaving their crisp packets and Coke cans behind them, the driver's seat pushed forward so little legs could reach the pedals. 'Ullo 'arry,' they'd say, their cheeky grins defying reprimand. One day I was accosted by their little eight-year-old girl;

'Alright, 'arry? What's that under your arm?'

'A book,' I replied.

'A book! What you gonna do with that?'

'I'm going to read it.'

'Aw!' Whenever I saw her after that she'd say 'Mornin', 'arry, still reading books?' and give a satisfied cluck at being acquainted with such an eccentric person. At about 6.30 their dad would come out, beer in hand, and yell from the balcony, 'Oi! Tea!' whereupon they'd all scuttle inside.

One day I came home to see Dad presenting an old Ford Cortina, which he'd obviously just acquired, to his family. The children were already swarming over it like the monkeys at Longleat and Mum was standing staring at it, arms crossed, with a glum look on her face, whilst Dad remon-

> 'Well I don't like brown, do I?' 'What's wrong with brown, then?' 'It's brown, innit.'

The

strated with her: 'What's wrong with it, then?'
'It's brown.'
'So what?'
'It is a brown car.'
'I know it's a brown car.'
'Well I don't like brown, do I?'
'What's wrong with brown, then?'
'It's brown, innit.'

This conversation went on for a good ten minutes, and became the inspiration for the first Slobs sketch, in which Wayne presented a brown car to the brown-hating Waynetta. I never dreamt that the characters would go on to be as popular as they were, but they did, and I'm proud of them.

Slobs

Wayne and Waynetta:
The Ten-Year

Int. Wayne and Waynetta's living room. Day. Wayne is sitting on the sofa. The dog is asleep on his lap. He is picking at her fur. Waynetta comes in.

Waynetta
Wayne!

Wayne
What?

Waynetta
What you doing?

Wayne
I'm de-fleaing Fergie.

Waynetta
Why?

Wayne
'Cos I'm hungry.

(He eats what he has picked from the dog.)

Waynetta
Wayne?

Wayne
What?

Waynetta
I want to split up.

Wayne
I'm not surprised, after the five pizzas you've just eaten.

Waynetta
No, I mean *us*. You and me.

Wayne
(Hurt) Oh ... Why? Don't you love me any more?

Waynetta
Of course I love you, Wayne. Love's got nothing to do with it. It's just ... we've been together ten years now and quite frankly it's unnatural.

Wayne
What is?

Waynetta
Being with someone that long. I'm the only mum on the estate with a live-in partner, all the other mums look at me like, you know, like I'm a bit of a tit.

(Wayne is open-mouthed. This is all a bit of a shock.)

Wayne
Well you are a bit of a tit, but not for that reason ...

Waynetta
I'm twenty-six years old, Wayne, I'm not getting any younger. I should be a single mother by now, it's embarrassing for the kids. They get teased by the others: 'You've got a daddy! You've got a daddy!' they sing. Frogmella came up to me the other day and said, 'Why haven't I got a brown sister like all the other kids?' Nearly broke my heart. All the other mums have got at least one brown baby, and I want one, and for that I need a big black man, and that ain't you, Wayne.

Itch

Wayne
But our kids are brown.

Waynetta
But that's not the same, is it, Wayne. That's dlrt. Oh lover, you're a good-looking bloke, you shouldn't be here. You should have had lots of different kids by now, by lots of different women, none of whom you ever see.

Wayne
I don't want lots of kids by different women. I love you and I love our kids.

Waynetta
Don't say that, Wayne! We're in enough trouble with the social services as it is. They came round here the other day and intergrated me about you.

Wayne
What d'they say?

Waynetta
They said, how come you lived here? How come you gave a toss about your kids? How come you stayed in at night and played

with the kids rather than going up the pub and getting pissed? They think you're a pervert, Wayne. You say you love 'em and they'll put 'em into care. You'd best go, lover.

Wayne
Where?

Waynetta
I dunno, be a homeless.

Wayne
I can't be a homeless. I'm too old to be a rent boy and too young to be a wino. I'm at that difficult age.

Waynetta
Well, I dunno. Something'll come up.

Wayne
Alright then, I'll go. *(Gets up)* I'll just kiss the kids goodbye.

Waynetta
Best not, they might tell someone.

Wayne
Oh ... Well goodbye for ever, then.

Waynetta
Goodbye for ever, lover.

Wayne
Love you.

Waynetta
And you ...

(Wayne leaves.

Cut to Wayne on the streets. He walks along. It is raining.

Cut to Wayne outside window of pizza parlour. He presses his face to window and salivates.

Cut to traffic lights. Wayne goes up to a car, spits on the windscreen and wipes it with his arm. He goes to the driver for money and gets a punch in the mouth.

Cut to Wayne walking up to a posh house. He knocks on the door. It is opened by top model Naomi Campbell.)

Naomi Campbell
Can I help you?

Wayne
Can I come and live in your house, please?

Naomi Campbell
Sure, come on in.

Wayne
Thank you.

(Cut to int. Naomi's house. It is posh.)

Wayne
Blimey!

Naomi Campbell
Hi, I'm Naomi Campbell, and I'm

a top model.

Wayne
I'm Wayne and I'm smelly.

Naomi Campbell
Let's get you washed, then.

(Cut to later. Naomi has a coat on and is doing lipstick in hall mirror. We hear Wayne off camera.)

Voice of Wayne
How do I look?

(Naomi turns to see.)

Naomi Campbell
Great!

(Wayne has black suit and black shirt on. Looks very trendy. His hair is pulled back into a ponytail. He gives a twirl and falls over.)

Naomi Campbell
Let's go eat.

(Cut to posh French restaurant. Naomi and Wayne at a table.)

Wayne
Blimey! It's all in foreign!

Naomi Campbell
Do you need some help with it?

Wayne
No, it's alright, I'll manage.

(The waiter comes up.)

Waiter
May I tek your orderzz?

Naomi Campbell
Yes please, I'd like the salade verte first, and then the fricassee de fruits de mer.

Waiter
Oui, and for Monsieur?

Wayne
I think I'll have the lot. The lot.

Waiter
Ze lot?

(Wayne gestures at the menu.)

Wayne
The lot.

(Cut to Naomi's bedroom. She shoves Wayne passionately on to the bed. He is stuffed.)

Naomi Campbell
Oh, Wayne darling!

Wayne
Ooof!

Naomi Campbell
You're so unlike all the other men!

Wayne
Erk!

Naomi Campbell
I love you!

Wayne
Fooof! Blimey!

(She starts to make love.

Cut to newspaper headlines: 'Naomi's New Hunk', 'Top model buys EEC food mountain for boyfriend', 'Naomi plumps for fat bastard'.

Cut to Wayne and Waynetta's living room. Waynetta reading last headline. She looks distressed.

Cut to Naomi's front door. Wayne opens door. Waynetta is standing on doorstep.)

Waynetta
Wayne?

Wayne
Waynetta! What are you doing here?

Waynetta
I want you back, Wayne. I'm jealous.

Wayne
Are yer?!!

Waynetta
Yeah, and I miss yer.

Wayne
Aw ... but I got a new bird now.

Waynetta
Well give her the boot!

Wayne
Yeah, but I ain't told her about us – what shall I say?

Waynetta
I dunno, make something up.

Wayne
I can't lie to her.

Waynetta
Wayne. You always lie to a bird when you give her the boot. It's the done thing.

Wayne
Alright then.

(Cut to Naomi's bedroom.)

Wayne
Nomeo?

Naomi Campbell
Yes, darling?

Wayne
I don't wanna go out with you no more.

Naomi Campbell
Why?

Wayne
Er ... You're too fat.

(Wayne turns round and runs.

Cut to ext. Naomi's house. Wayne bursts out door.)

Wayne
Quick, leg it.

(They leg it.

Cut to caption: 'A year or two later'. Cut to Wayne and Waynetta's living room. The doorbell goes. They look at each other.)

Wayne
Get that.

Waynetta
You get it!

Wayne
You get it!

Waynetta
You get it!

Wayne
You get it!

Waynetta
You get it!

(She boots Wayne off sofa. He gets up and goes to the door.)

Wayne
You get it!

Waynetta
Get it!

Wayne
Get it!

Waynetta
GET IT!!

(Wayne answers door.

Outside is Naomi.)

Wayne
Yeah? Oh, hullo.

Naomi Campbell
Hello, Wayne.

Wayne
Alright?

Naomi Campbell
Listen, Wayne, you know that affair we had?

Wayne
Yeah.

Naomi Campbell
Well you got me in the club, and I had octuplets – d'you want one?

(Wayne looks down: we see eight babies.)

Wayne
Blimey! Er, hang on a sec.

(Wayne hurries in to Waynetta.)

Wayne
Waynetta?

Waynetta
Wot!

Wayne
If we had another kid, would you want a boy or a girl?

Waynetta
I want a likkle boy, dunnoi?

Why?

Wayne
Oh nothIng.

(He hurries back to Naomi.)

Wayne
Got any boys?

Naomi Campbell
Yes, two. That one and that one.

Wayne
I'll have that one please.

(Naomi gives him the baby.)

Naomi Campbell
His names's Wayne.

Wayne
Right, thanks very much.

(He shuts door and returns with baby.)

Wayne
Waynetta!

Waynetta
Wot!

Wayne
Got you a present, innoi.

(Gives her the baby.)

Waynetta
Oh, Wayne! My very own brown baby! Oh, now I'm like all the other mums on the estate!

(They look at baby and kiss horribly with tongues.

Cut to ext. Grotty council estate. Night. Pan up to a high flat with lights on. We hear the voices of Wayne and Waynetta shouting.)

Waynetta
He's called Canoe!!

Wayne
He's called Wayne!!

Waynetta
He's called Canoe!!

Wayne
He's called Wayne!!

Waynetta
He's called Canoe
Reeves Slob!!

Wayne
He's called Wayne!!

Waynetta
(Not shouting)
Wayne?

Wayne
What?

(We hear the noise of metal against flesh.)

Wayne
Ow!!

There is always an element of luck in getting to know the 'right person at the right time'. For me, a friend of Charlie Higson (who was then a cult pop star) had a friend called Mary who had a friend called Helen who had a friend called Anthony who arranged for me to have lunch in 1984 with John Lloyd, Britain's top comedy producer at the time, who had invented *Not The Nine O'Clock News*, as well as producing *Blackadder.* I took him a script I'd written a year before called *Norbert Smith*, a satire of the British film industry. I read it to him and he laughed, but said he was too busy to do anything with my script as he was making *Spitting Image* – which had then just finished its first series. 'Oh, can I do *Spitting Image*?' I asked. 'Can you do impressions?' he replied. 'No, but I'll learn.'

So I learnt some impressions over the summer, recorded myself on my home cassette as Jimmy Greaves, Arthur Scargill and others, and sent John Lloyd the tape. I then rang him and asked if I could come and see the *Spitting Image* workshops, in Limehouse, East London. I went there several times and spent the autumn sucking up to Roger Law and Peter Fluck, the puppet caricaturists. I also told all my friends I was doing the next series of the programme, even though I hadn't yet been given the job and didn't know if I'd get it. I did this to make sure that I didn't get lazy about pestering John, I'd *have* to get the job or all my friends would think I was a mad fantasizing prat. Then, the day before the first programme of the new series was to go out, John finally rang.

'We've got a sketch with Jimmy Greaves in it – would you mind awfully coming up to Birmingham to record tomorrow? I'm sorry it's such short notice, and I'm afraid we can only pay you the Equity minimum of £174.50.' Did I mind! £174.50 for one day's work! I was on the first train to Birmingham, and having got my foot in the door, I was determined to shove it open. I sucked up to everyone, wrote hundreds of dodgy scripts for *Spitting Image*, all of which were politely turned down by the script editors, Rob Grant and Doug Naylor (who later went on to write and make *Red Dwarf*), except one – a sketch with Prince Philip popping round the corner of Buckingham Palace for a kebab from his brother's kebab shop. This sketch they accepted, and I played Bubelos, Philip's brother. A few months later that sketch was to get me a job on the programme that would make my name – *Saturday Night Live.*

So you could say that if I hadn't known Charlie Higson, who knew Mary, who had a friend called Helen, whose boss Anthony knew John Lloyd, I'd never have got my break. But as well as the luck, I did do a lot of work and an even larger amount of sucking up to the right people once I'd met them!

In 1976, when I was fifteen, something odd happened in music – the punk revolution. Before then there were a few big supergroups. Then suddenly there were groups like the Pistols and the Clash. By 1977 hundreds of little bands with their own record labels were playing pubs and clubs, not stadiums. You didn't have to be a brilliant musician to be in a band, you just had to want to do it. You didn't need a smart record executive to sign you up to a posh label – you could play your local pubs, and put out your own records.

In 1979, a similar thing happened in comedy. Before then 'alternative' (i.e. not family sitcom) comedy was restricted to the 'supergroups' like the Monty Python team, Pete and Dud and *Not The Nine O'Clock News* team. It seemed to young people that to do comedy you had to have been in the Cambridge University Footlights or the Oxford University equivalent. Then the

10 Per Cent

Comedy Store opened in London, fronted by new young comics like Alexei Sayle, Rik Mayall, Ade Edmondson, Dawn French and Jennifer Saunders. At the Comedy Store, *anyone* could get up and try to be a comic. The success of the Comedy Store led to hundreds of new comedy clubs sprouting up – above pubs, in disused churches – where anyone could 'get up and have a go', and if they were successful, would be *paid*

to perform there again. Since '79 the TV comics who've started by just getting up at clubs on the comedy circuit and having a go include not only those mentioned above, but also me, Jack Dee, Mark Lamarr, Lee Evans, Reeves and Mortimer, Paul Merton, Lee Hurst and nearly everyone else.

My personal experience was to fall into comedy by mistake. When I was at university, I went to see a comedy play at the local Arts

Luck

Centre which was extremely funny, mainly because of one actor, a fellow student called Bryan Elsley. About a year later, I got to know Bryan and we found we made each other laugh. We went to see two comedy plays together, one by The National Theatre of Brent and one by Cliffhanger, both of which were funnier than anything either of us had seen since Monty Python. On a high from seeing these plays, Bryan asked me if I'd like to write and perform a similar type of show to the two-hander that was The National Theatre of Brent for the small University Theatre. I was flattered to be asked, but nervous of acting with the funniest performer at university when I hadn't been on a stage since school plays years before, but I said I would. We wrote *Dusty and Dick's Lucky Escape from the Germans*, a *Great Escape* spoof, and performed it to the university audience, where it went well, and Bryan suggested that he use some of the money he'd been left by his late father to stage the show at 1982's Edinburgh Festival, two months after our Finals. As I didn't know what the hell I was going to do with my life after university, I was pleased to have something to work towards at least for the next few months.

We performed at the Celtic Lodge, a sixty-seat room, to twelve people for the first couple of nights, but then got a good review from the *Edinburgh Evening News* and pretty much sold out for the rest of the run. On about the fourth day, a BBC radio producer, Paul Mahew Archer, came to the show and asked us if we wanted to write for radio. Despite Paul having flared trousers, we agreed.

So after Edinburgh we came to London and tried to write for radio. Nearly all our sketches were rejected, but we still earnt a few quid. Not knowing what else to do with our lives, we thought we'd keep writing jokes. We joined a Government 'New Business' scheme, our business being Dusty and Dick Productions, purveyors of fine comedy. We got £40 a week, plus whatever we earnt from the BBC. We also wrote an act for the flourishing comedy circuit, and after doing 'open spots' in venues all over London, quickly established ourselves as regular performers. The Government business scheme provided funds for a year, and I decided I'd keep doing comedy for that period, then probably have to get a proper job. My parents were quietly baffled by what I was doing, but my father, whilst not interfering lest I bite his head off, did suggest that perhaps he might buy me a suit for job interviews, should I ever feel the desire to seek proper employment. Knowing it would make him happy, I consented, and we duly went down to his tailor in Chichester, who ran me up a very respectable suit that would have opened many a door for me in the City. That suit was never to see an office,

My parents were quietly baffled by what I was doing, but my father, whilst not interfering lest I bite his head off, did suggest that perhaps he might buy me a suit for job interviews

but was to be doused by beer in many a rowdy club around Britain over the next two years. Its last outing was when Bryan and I supported the Stranglers on tour, where my poor, respectable business suit was doused in the phlegm of a thousand spitting punks each night as we were booed off the stage.

Dusty and Dick were a pretty successful cabaret act – by the end of 1984 we were topping the bill in all the new London clubs – but wider success was not to happen. Our first appearance on TV was selling clothes to Dawn French in her fashion show *Swank*. We also came bottom of a poll on a TV talent show called *The Fame Game,* beaten by a comedy songwriter, a Bilko impressionist and a chap with a squeaky voice.

In 1985, I decided we'd taken Dusty and Dick as far as it would go, and that I wanted to perform on my own. When we'd started, Bryan had been very much the senior partner of the act, financing our first show at Edinburgh and giving me encouragement and confidence. But Bryan's performance skills were very different to mine. He excelled in front of a theatre audience, where a large stage provided the space for his 'physical' comedy. My comedy was more accent- and character-based, which was much more suited to the tiny Comedy Club stages, which were often little more than a couple of upturned beer crates and a microphone. I'm much bossier than Bryan, and after he'd given me my confidence, I began to manipulate him into letting our cabaret act lean far more towards showing off my comedy skills than his own. By '85 I felt confident enough to go it alone. When I started, I'd needed Bryan to 'hold my hand', but now I could walk, I ditched him. Bryan directed my solo 'Loadsamoney and Stavros' show in 1988, and is now a highly successful TV and film screenwriter – *The Crow Road* is one of his many, more recent, credits.

From 1982 to 1986 I lived on the top floor of a council block in Hackney, East London. My next-door neighbour was Charlie Higson, and Paul Whitehouse lived in the adjacent block. Our local pub was the Brunswick, in Well Street, opposite which was Adam's kebab shop. Adam Athanassiou's shop was like the local youth club – always full of teenagers playing the pac-man video game. Hackney youth being Hackney youth, fights were frequently in the air, but Adam always managed to keep the peace with humour, deflecting the aggression on to himself: 'You two cheeky monkey-sod! Plis kindly stop behave like your bottems are on top of your neck. If you don't,' said little bald Adam, 'you know I am really Silly Vester Stallone in disguise innit, and I'm a goin' to have to bop your stupid heads together.' As Adam would say, 'If a atmosphere is become unpleas' I tell a joke, and Bob, he is your uncle. Everybody is happy again.' He was incredibly popular, and we all used to imitate him. Paul did the best impression (as usual), but had no ambition to hit the stage at the time, being a well-paid plasterer. After I stopped doing Dusty and Dick with Bryan Elsley, I needed characters for my solo stand-up. From his kebab shop, Adam gave us great insights into the goings-on of local Hackney life. I decided a kebab shop owner would be an ideal character for insights into national life.

I called the character Stavros after Kojak's brother – Kojak being the best-known Greek on television. Stavros made his first appearance at a benefit concert for a Colombian earthquake appeal in 1985. It was at the Albert Hall, in front of 5,000 people. I started my new routine to total silence. Within a minute the audience was booing, and within two I had been slow-handclapped off the stage. Before I'd gone on I'd been pacing around backstage nervously going through my lines – being about to try out a new character in front of the biggest audience I'd ever played to concentrated my mind somewhat, and I was thus totally unaware of who was on stage before me. I was told afterwards that it had been a Colombian, who had just told the audience that he had lost several of his family in the earthquake. Then I had gone on and, the acoustics of the Albert Hall not being brilliant for Greek-cockney speech, no one could hear what the hell I was going on about, but the universal impression was that I was taking the piss out of this poor fellow who'd lost his family. Talk about bad taste. Ho hum, that's showbiz, folks.

Saturday Night Live started in the January of the next year, 1986, with various regular acts including Rik Mayall and Ade Edmondson, Fry and Laurie and Ben Elton. I was daunted by the new company I was keeping, especially by Fry and Laurie, both of whom were very tall, very posh and very, very clever. Ben Elton, characteristically, made me feel at ease by christening me 'Junior Boy', a name I kept for the next three series. He roared with laughter the first time Stavros appeared in rehearsals for the show, which gave me a huge confidence-boost – it was a year later before he confessed he'd thought my performance was rubbish. Looking back at my

Stavr

first show, Ben was right – the sketch I did was utterly feeble, but for some reason the producers stuck with me, and over the next twenty-five shows I gradually built up confidence and my popularity grew accordingly.

Stavros is probably my personal favourite solo character (Wayne and Kevin are my favourite 'double-act characters). When Paul, Charlie and Geoff Perkins came in on the writing team in 1987, I enjoyed doing him even more. I enjoyed his individualistic command of the English language, which gave him the ability to appear wide-eyed and innocent whilst taking a cheeky swipe at the good and the great. Hence Mrs Thatcher became 'The Ironing Lady' – just a bit wrong, but not the image she would have liked. Then there was the leader of the opposition, Mr Kin cock, who was always 'kin cockIng things up'. Even now, nine years later, I still get more requests to 'bring back Stavros' than any other character I've killed off.

If a atmosphere is become unpleas' I tell a joke, and Bob, he is your uncle. Everybody is happy again

OS

Loadsamoney

For the first programme of *Friday Night Live* in early 1988, I tried out a new character at the end of the show. He was a plasterer but neither myself, nor Paul, Charlie or Geoffrey could think of a name that would suit him. We tried Dave, Kev, Geoff and Tony, but none of them seemed right. So he became known in rehearsals that week as 'Harry's new bloke'. I did my Stavros monologue near the beginning of the show, then went backstage to change. In my snow-washed jeans and bad-taste ski jacket, with highlights in my hair, and a wad of cut-up newspaper with a ten pound note stuck at each end, I was ready. When Ben Elton finally introduced me on to the stage, he said, 'Now, Ladies and Gentlemen, a new character from the man who brought you Stavros. Will you please welcome – the Plasterer!' I walked on stage and yelled, 'Look at that! Look at my wad! I've got loadsamoney!' For three minutes I swanked about the stage boasting about all my money. Within days the Plasterer had become a tabloid anti-hero – and they'd given him a name: 'Loadsamoney'.

Loadsamoney, or 'Loads' as he became known, was not only the character that really made me famous, but was also the most fun to do. He owed his existence to a large extent to Paul Whitehouse. Paul was a plasterer himself at the time, writing bits of Stavros for me as a sideline. One day about a year before *Friday Night Live*, Paul and I were standing on the platform of Caledonian Road Station, waiting for a train. I noticed that lying on the ground on the opposite platform was a copper pipe encased in rubber insulation. I said to Paul, 'See that pipe? You wanna smelt it down, doncha?'

'Oh yes,' said Paul, sagely. 'You wanna smelt that down alright. You wanna take it home. Bosh! In the Black & Decker Home Smelter. Shoom! Rubber bubbles up the top. Doink! You gotcher self a nice bit of copper. There's money in copper, loadsamoney!'

By the time our train arrived, he'd smelted down all the ironwork on the station, another passenger's umbrella, the chocolate vending machine and the train track. On the journey home he smelted down the train, a gasworks, two buses and a passing 747: 'Lookadat plane up there – you wanna smelt that down alright. Bosh! Nice bit steel oxide type thing. Oh there's money in steel oxide type thing alright, it's a highly sought-after product. Oh yes, oh yes, oh yes – loadsamoney in that.'

A week later, when I saw Paul down the pub, it was clear he'd been smelting things down all week, for now not only him, but Charlie Higson, who was painting the walls Paul plastered, and Paul's boss Martin were also smelting everything down – including the Prime Minister, Mrs Thatcher: 'You know that Maggie Thatcher? The Iron Lady? They wanna smelt her down, don't they? Get a nice, soft ladylike ore, lovely! There's a lot of demand for your ladylike ore from the modern architects – they pay loadsamoney!'

I was looking for a new character for my 1987 Edinburgh show and I felt there was something in Paul's Smelt Down Man. I liked the whole wide-boy, there's-money-in-everything attitude, and thought that instead of Smelt Down Man, he should be a plasterer like Paul. We were at the height of the mid-eighties housing boom, and plasterers saw themselves as the aristocracy of builders. Paul's boss, Martin, was a 'mouldings' plasterer – the *crème de la crème* of his trade. After all the other builders had been sweating away for weeks on a house, Martin would waltz in at the last minute, repair and renew the old Victorian cornicing and swan off in his Porsche, having earnt more than the rest of the tradesmen put together. I thought my character should be like this, but unlike Martin, who is a quiet bloke who keeps himself to himself, my bloke would be more like one of the blokes in our local. In the Brunswick pub in Hackney our little group, which included Paul and Charlie, were known by the other locals as the 'student hippie squatting wankers' – even though none of us were students, or hippies, or squatters. But we didn't have highlights in our hair, or snow-washed jeans – and we were obviously middle-class – so it was assumed by the others that we must be squatters. They'd overhear us saying things like 'Could you lend us a fiver till Monday?' and realized that, whoever we were, they were better off than us. When it came to ordering drinks, there was one chap who always sidled up to our side of the bar, ostentatiously took out a huge wad of notes from his back pocket and nonchalantly chucked a twenty pound note on the bar as if it was so much dirt. He'd glance round at us to make sure we'd clocked him and give us a 'you-may-be-ponces-but-I-got-more-money-than-you' smirk.

So I wanted my character to be a plasterer, like Paul and Martin, with the look-at-the-size-of-my-wad attitude of Brunswick Bloke.

We gave Smelt Down Man Martin's mouldings job and a Brunswick-Bloke-size wad, but

'Look at that! Look at my wad! I've got loadsamoney!

instead of flashing it by-mistake-on-purpose, our bloke flaunted his money. 'Look at my wad! I got loadsamoney! I'm a plasterer innol? Bosh bosh shoom shoom lovely job LOADSAMONEY. Wey hey hey! I got more money than you, you paupers! Bow down you scum and worship my wad! Har har har! You're poor, I'm not! Loadsamoney! Did I tell you I'm richer than you? 'Cos I am! Look! Loadsamoney.'

The new character went well in Edinburgh. Then I did him on the cabaret circuit in London and finally on *Friday Night Live*. I never expected him to be taken up by the press in the way he was. He became a symbol of eighties Britain. And he was the greatest fun to do live, because I could just get up on stage and be naughty!

One night, I did a benefit gig at Ealing Town Hall for the nurses, who were on strike in an attempt to get their pay increased. Before I went on, various 'right-on' stand-up comics did their acts, getting huge rounds of applause for all their anti-Tory and anti-Thatcher jokes. Then it was my turn. Loadsamoney walked on stage, surveyed the audience with contempt and shouted, 'GET BACK TO WORK YOU SCUM!' I pranced around the stage telling them what wankers they were, how great BUPA was, how they should close the NHS down and develop the hospitals into flats for me to plaster. I explained what fun it was overtaking an ambulance with its siren on in my Escort XR3i Turbo Nutter Bastard, then shoving my brakes on so the ambulance screeched to a halt, causing the ill bloke's stretcher to zoom forward into the cabin and knock the driver's head through his windscreen – arf, arf! The nurses were asking for a seven-pound-a-week-rise – so I took out a tenner and burnt it on stage. I was as politically incorrect as I could possibly be and the nurses loved it. The more I insulted them, the more they laughed. I don't think I've ever enjoyed a gig as much as that one.

The Death of Loads

Loadsamoney first appeared on television in February 1988. In February 1989, I 'killed him off' – he was run over and killed on *Comic Relief*. It was mainly because he was so one-dimensional that I couldn't think of anything new for him to do. After ten 3-minute slots on *Friday Night Live*, Paul, Charlie and I wrote a 20-minute set for my live tour in autumn '88, and it all seemed to be about spending cash and shagging. It wasn't very good, and every night I did him on stage, he'd go down brilliantly for the first five minutes and then the laughs would tail off swiftly. I'd basically run out of good ideas for him. Secondly, I wanted to move on. Harry Enfield was known almost exclusively as Stavros and Loadsamoney, and I wanted to try lots of new characters. New characters always take some time to become popular (Stavros took a year) and people like best what they already know. So for Wayne and Waynetta, the Gits, Tim Nice But Dim and all the other new creations to have a chance of working, I felt Stav and Loads would have to go.

'GET BACK TO WORK YOU SCUM!'

At the height of *Friday Night Live*'s success I decided to do Loads' Northern equivalent. The eighties boom seemed very much a Southern phenomenon. Touring round the country doing gigs, I was aware of the North–South divide – the South full of yuppies and new housing, the North full of derelict industries and closed-down mines. I'd spent a lot of time in Newcastle, doing gigs and spots on Channel Four's *The Tube*. I loved the Geordie people, their pride in their city and their sense of humour. I'd also hung around with the boys who wrote *Viz* comic, which was then just taking off. I really wanted to do a character for the North to counteract Loads the Southerner. So Paul, Charlie, Geoff Perkins, Chris and I cobbled a sketch together. The accent was the next big thing – the Geordie accent is not the easiest to learn for a 'Southern puff' like me. So I had to send Chris Donald, the editor of *Viz*, a copy of the script in Newcastle. He then rang up my answering machine and read it out phonetically on to the tape, which I played to myself again and again until I'd got the voice as best I could.

He worked fine on the programme, and the Geordies I met in the street were very nice about him – but said my accent was crap! They said I sounded 'like a bloody Mak'em'. I'd never heard the word 'Mak'em' and it turned out to mean someone from Sunderland – Geordies like to think that their neighbours are thickheads, good only for ordering about: 'Yer mak'em dee this and mak'em dee that.'

The word was to come in handy when I faced my biggest Buggerallmoney challenge – doing a gig in Newcastle where I had to face two thousand pissed-up Geordies on their home turf. Buggerallmoney came on to huge applause, but as soon as I've gone, 'I've got bugger-allmoney and I'm a Geordie me!' I had howls of abuse from the back of the hall: 'You're not a Geordie, yer big Southern puff.' Immediately I hit back: 'How mon! Yer say Ah'm norra Geordie. Worrad yees know aboot that? Yer dorty greet Mak'em!!' Just knowing the word 'Mak'em' saved my bacon – I got a huge laugh and the hecklers left me in peace. I zoomed through my set as fast as I could, hoping that the quicker the words came out, the better they would sound, but at the end of the evening I asked the audience how my accent had been and two thousand people yelled in unison: 'SHITE !!'

I asked the audience how my accent had been and two thousand people yelled in unison: 'SHITE!!!'

Buggerallmoney

Norbert Smith

After the success of Loadsamoney and Stavros on *Saturday Night Live*, I didn't know what I wanted to do, other than something different. The only project I had in any sort of pipeline was 'Norbert Smith', the spoof of the British film industry I'd written after university, which we eventually sold to Channel Four.

Norbert Smith was a fictional actor who we used to satirize British cinema from its beginnings to the present day. I love old British films and we made spoofs of such genres as the fifties 'kitchen sink' dramas like *Look Back in Anger* with *It's Grim Up North* – 'I'm going out to fly me bloody whippets!' – and Carry On films with *Carry On Banging*, where Barbara Windsor is the leader of the feminists trying to get rid of nuclear weapons from Greenham airbase: 'We want you to pull out your big ones and if you don't, we will,' etc.

Norbert Smith also appeared in a wartime documentary telling soldiers about the dangers of venereal disease – but because they were so straight-laced in the 1940s he had to do it without mentioning sex or people's private parts: 'Venereal disease is caused by ghastly horridness, beastly nastiness and sordid frightfulness and leads to unpleasantness on the unmentionables.' This sketch was the forerunner to to all the Mr Chomondley-Warner sketches. Throughout *Norbert Smith* the eighty-year-old Sir Norbert was interviewed at home by Melvyn Bragg, who did such a good job he was nominated for Best Comedy Performance at the Comedy Awards!

Fat Bloke

Fat Bloke first appeared in a Lee and Lance sketch in my first series: 'Alright, Lee? Lance?' 'Alright, Fat Bloke?' He was on and off the screen in seconds, but I got a lot of people saying to me, 'Where's Fat Bloke, then?' for months afterwards. So in the second series we put him in every show. He was a sort of 'roving extra'. Tim Nice But Dim would be with the bank manager and Fat Bloke would come in and put a cup of tea on the manager's desk: 'Thank you, Fat Bloke,' 'Alright, bank manager,' and off he'd go until next week, when he'd pop up in The Scousers.

Fat Bloke – or David, as he's really called – was game for anything, so in the third series we had him at the end of each show: 'The show's not over until the Fat Bloke sings,' whereupon he'd sing something odd like 'Lord Of The Dance' or 'Nkosi Sikewe i'Africa', the South African National Anthem. I should have used him in my last series, but forgot until it was too late. Stupid me, I like Fat Bloke, he's our lucky mascot.

Smashie and Nicey are in my opinion the best characters Paul and I have done together. For ages I'd thought about doing a disc jockey and so had Paul. He'd first done Mike Smash on a show for Jonathan Ross a year before he made his debut on my show. It seemed odd to me that, although millions of people listened to Radio 1 every day, no comedian had ever taken off their DJs before us.

It had always struck Paul and me that there were two main types of DJs – those who loved music, like John Peel and Alan Freeman, and those who loved the sound of their own voices, like DLT. Many of the latter type clearly couldn't care less about music – Peel told me that he once went to dinner at a top Radio 1 DJ's house and was amazed to see that he had no record-, cassette- or CD-player – no music in the house at all! Of course, some DJs overlap both types, like Tony Blackburn, who loved a good yatter but still had a passion and expert knowledge of music, especially soul music.

Radio 1 also struck us as a funny old place because, in 1990, when we started doing the DJs, the whole youth culture was ultra-modern, with the take-off of dance music and fashion-conscious, music-based magazines like *Q*, but Radio 1 was still dominated by DJs with seventies haircuts and cuddly cardigans, whose idea of a good record was Rolf Harris's 'Tie Me Kangaroo Down'.

Smashie and Nicey were lots of DJs moulded together. Mike Smash was 'daft' (Noel Edmonds), loved a really bad joke (Tony Blackburn), always seemed a bit tragic (Mike Reed), had a dreadful hair-do (all of them except Peel) and appeared to be much more interested in himself than music (Gary Davies). Plus, when he tried to 'be serious for a minute' he sounded silly (Simon Bates).

I wanted Nicey to be as different from Smash as possible. Although I had an Alan Freeman-type voice and a liking for 'rock' (though, unlike Freeman, I really shared Smashie's lack of interest in music), I had a different sort of character in mind. I wanted him to think he was 'mad' and 'daft' but in fact be totally humourless and incredibly pompous. I wanted Nicey to think that because the odd looney wrote to him telling him he was great, he thought that the whole nation was in awe of him, hanging on to every one of his idiotic thoughts. I wanted him to be mean-spirited, not a very nice man.

But the first time I did him in the studio, the audience just found him too unpleasant. So we had to go back to the drawing board and make him into a cuddly old buffoon, always going on about his 'young friend', though never admitting he was gay, and talking rubbish with Smashie to his heart's content. It was only in my special, *Smashie and Nicey – The End of an Era*, that I allowed the true, nasty Nicey, to really come out.

We did *Smashie and Nicey – The End of an Era* because, with Radio 1's then controller, Matthew Bannister, getting rid of the bulk of Radio 1's old guard, it seemed time to lay our guys to rest. They both came to a sad end, and after the show had been on TV, Simon Bates saw Paul and asked him how we had got everything so uncannily accurate – who was our 'inside source' at Radio 1 who'd told us about certain DJs' breakdowns? But we didn't have a source – we just did what we thought was right for our characters. The fact that it happened to reflect the secret real lives of some DJs shouldn't really come as a surprise – most Radio 1 DJs had worn their hearts on their sleeves for decades.

The End of an Era is probably the piece of work I'm personally most proud of. My only regret

Smashie and

is the sketch where Smashie's marriage breaks down. This was a 'satire' of Tony Blackburn's marriage break-up, if you can call it satire. It was in fact cheap and cruel, and Mr Blackburn, who's never harmed anyone, didn't deserve his private life to be mocked. I am deeply ashamed of this sketch, as is Paul.

Radio 1 was still dominated by DJs with seventies haircuts and cuddly cardigans

Nicey

Smashie and Nicey

Smashie
Fab-four-tastic! That was the, err, Beatles, err – I love the Beatles, don't you? – with 'Eight Days A Week'.

Nicey
There's only seven days in a week, mate.

Smashie
Right, thanks, mate.

Nicey
Don't mention it.

Smashie
Erm, but I think you'll find that's what the Beatles – I love the Beatles, don't you? – were saying –

Nicey
I don't care what the Beatles – I love the Beatles, don't you? – were saying, mate, there's only seven days in a week, never longer, never shorter. It's the law!

Smashie
Right!

Nicey
Right, starts on a Monday, goes through to a Sunday, with a Wednesday, Friday type stuff in the middle, and the weekend on the end.

Smashie
I love the weekend, don't you mate?

Nicey
Me too, mate.

Smashie
Right, well one thing I do know, is that err, today, is err, Tuesday which is quite literally, err – Tuesday.

Nicey
I love Tuesdays, don't you mate?

Smashie
Certainly do, mate. It's one of the best between Monday and Wednesday type days we've got.

Nicey
It's the only between Monday and Wednesday type day we've got, mate. It may not have the glamour and excitement of a Saturday, or the mournfulness of a Monday morn, but it's our Tuesday, the good, old-fashioned, honest to goodness, down to earth, great British Tuesday, and if those Eurocrats, Bureaucrats and other Bonkerscrats try and take our Tuesday away from us, they'll have to get past me first. And if they think I'm gonna start me show by saying Bonjourno doo-dle-doo, and Guten Morgen mongous, they've got another think coming.

Smashie
I don't think they are gonna do that, mate. It'd be frogadobad-abulously bonkers, mate. Because what makes a nation is not its borders or its monetary system, no, it's its radio stations, such as Radio Fab F.M., and the people who work there-in. Such as you, Nicey. You are what makes Britain great.

Nicey
Thanks mate. *(Pause)* Err, so are you, mate.

Smashie
Thanks, mate, because this European business is really getting out of hand, I mean, now we've got all these daft new countries making themselves up and wanting to be part of Europe, and err, I can't keep track of 'em.

Nicey
Well there's Ruromania, Czechoslavia, Hungerslavia, Mongerslavia,

Obstobstobamory, Orinocho and Bulgaria.

Smashie
Whatever did 'appen to the Wombles, mate?

Nicey
Good point, mate, one certainly worth making – what happened to the Wombles? Well, I'll tell ya, they were underground, overground wombling free and then … no, mate … they were … were they? … not here …where they were … type stuff.

Smashie
Wombling wise words, mate.

Nicey
Thanks, mate.

Smashie
I loved the Wombles. They really were in a sort of short pro-gramme before the news sort of way.

Nicey
They cer-tainly were, mate.

Smashie
And err, I think we've all got a little bit of the Wombles in us, haven't we and err, I bet you've got a bit of the Womble in you, haven't you, Nicey?

Nicey
Well, err, I do know the Pet Shop Boys, if that's what you mean.

Smashie
Not really no, err, in fact, err, I think it's time I was making a move because I'm taking over from Pip Schofield tonight in *Joseph's Coat*. So, this is me, Mike no stranger to charity Smash, saying arrividercl-doo-dle-doo.

Nicey
Auf Wiedersehen Pet. Alright you Euro-prats, listen to me. My name is Davenport Nice and I'm a-standing, yes Davenport, I'm a-standing firm for Britain, for her Tuesdays, for her Wombles, for her Bachman, for her Turner and most of all her noble Overdrive. You ain't seen nothing yet, Euro Poppers. Let us rock.

Smashie
Nicey?

Nicey
Mate?

Smashie
Do you really know the Pet Shop Boys?

Nicey
I know the quiet one, mate.

charlie Higson

I first met Charlie when I was sixteen and went to stay with Dave Cummings, the elder brother of my schoolfriend Ted, in Norwich. Dave shared a house with Charlie, who impressed me enormously, because he lived with a girl (I was still at snogging stage), called himself 'Switch' and had dyed black hair. But what impressed me most was that he refused to talk to me all weekend, ignoring me or directing the odd snarl in my direction if I dared to try to converse with him. I thought he was really cool. His pop group, the Higsons, got 'record of the week' in the *New Musical Express* with their single 'I Don't Want To Live With Monkeys', which made him even cooler, and for the next few years he lived the life of a touring 'indie' band member. (I was once the Higsons' van-driver – driving them to a gig in Aberystwyth.) After the split up of the Higsons, 'Switch' became 'Murray' for a while, and started painting and decorating the walls Paul plastered. Then, in 1987, he became 'Charlie', and started writing with Paul for me. Charlie co-wrote much of the material I did on *Saturday Night Live* with Paul and myself, and like Paul came on tour with me to get his Equity card. Charlie's job on tour was to start the second half of the show after the interval, as the worst support act in history, who I would then come on and shoot dead. So that the audience would think he was genuine, he was billed on the tour posters as 'Noel Clore with his comedy songs'. Paul, Charlie and I have always hated comedy songs – they are nearly always embarrassingly unfunny. Noel Clore came on stage in a wacky hat and said, 'Hiya! My name's Noel Clore – Grrr! Ha ha!' The audience would look at him in stunned silence. He'd continue, 'Anyway, you know what it's like how there always seem to be lots of extra coathangers in your wardrobe? Yeah?' More silence from the audience and the odd yell of 'No!' and 'You what?' 'Ha ha! Well anyway!' he'd continue, 'I dunno, it's as if coathangers had babies in the night when you're asleep, isn't it? Ha ha!' 'Get off,' people would start to yell, but Charlie kept up his act brilliantly. 'Well anyway, here's a song about all those little coathangers. Hope you like it.' On a good night he'd be being slow-handclapped by the time he launched into his song: 'Oh, coathangers hangin' in yer wardrobe! Coathangers hangin' on yer wall! Coathangers hangin' on yer ceiling! Coathangers hangin' in yer hall!' He'd plough on, all naïve smiles amidst the yelling of the audience, until I came on as Sir Henry and shot him dead, to rapturous applause. Noel Clore could not have been less cool or more embarrassingly performed. He was a far cry from Charlie's last stage performance, as 'Switch', lead singer of the Higsons.

Charlie continued to write for my next two series, but I wouldn't let him perform. 'Charlie, you can't be in this sketch because you're crap!' I'd say, regularly. I don't know why I thought he'd be crap after his brilliant performance as Noel Clore. His subsequent excellent *Fast Show* characters have proved how wrong I was.

'Anyway, you know what it's like how there always seem to be lots of extra coathangers in your wardrobe? Yeah?'

Coming from a middle-class background, where books and education were considered badges of honour, I was brought up to believe that your character was more important than your possessions.

Often when I'm in my car I've had a much posher car pull up next to me at the lights. I'll see the driver give my car a contemptuous once-over. He'll also notice with pleasure that I'm looking at his car and a flicker of a smirk will come over his face as he takes in what he thinks is my envy. I always think the icing on the cake would be if he wound down his window and said, 'S'cuse me, mate! I'm considerably richer than you!'

People who think they're better than other people just because they've got more money, a better car, a Rolex watch, always strike me as funny. Stanley and Pam Herbert are the ultimate *nouveaux riches* – they don't just think they're better than everyone else, they tell everyone they are. They're older versions of Loadsamoney. I don't hate snobs, I just think they're silly, and Stanley and Pam are very silly, especially Pam, who Kathy plays with a fantastically vacant grin that means I can't look at her when we're filming – if I do, I start to giggle. In my last series I had them with Pammy's sister and brother-in-law. I know many families where one of the sisters marries someone rich and starts getting above herself and patronizing her siblings. It seemed a fun area to take the characters into. But the sketch here is the first one we did, in a restaurant, where the uncultured Herberts boast to a pair of educated, but poorer, teachers.

'Oi, you lot! Look at me! I'm considerably richer than you!'

CONSIDERABLY RICHER THAN YOU

A Spanish restaurant in Spain. Two tables. At one are the Herberts. At the other table are the Parkers. They are obviously very much in love. The Herberts are observing them.

Considerably Richer Than You

Stanley Herbert
Excuse me, sport! I hope you don't mind me interrupting!

Mr Parker
No, er, that's OK.

Stanley Herbert
Only, the wife and I noticed that we happen to be considerably richer than you.

Mr Parker
I'm sorry?

Stanley Herbert
We appear to be considerably richer than you.

Mr Parker
Is that a fact?

Pam Herbert
Oh yes, I mean, just look at our clothes: we wear Chanel and Pierre Cardin. Our friends here wear Next and C&A.

Stanley Herbert
Thank you Pam! Proof indeed that we are considerably richer than you!

Mr Parker
Lucky old you.

Stanley Herbert
Luck!!

Pam Herbert
Luck!!

Stanley Herbert
Luck!!

Pam Herbert
Luck!!

Stanley Herbert
Did you say luck? No, luck's got nothing to do with it!

Pam Herbert
Luck!!

Stanley Herbert
No No!! I became considerably richer than you by honest hard work. You get what you pay for

and you earn what you're worth!

Pam Herbert
That's one of Stanley's little sayings, that is. Do you know, my Stanley probably makes more money in a year than you do in ten!

Stanley Herbert
What do you think of that then, sport?

Mr Parker
Gosh!

Stanley Herbert
Now correct me if I'm wrong, but isn't every financial decision you make a struggle?

Mr Parker
Look.

Stanley Herbert
Not for us it isn't! Oh, yes, money's done me proud. I mean just look at my wife. I mean, nothing dowdy about my Pammy, is there? No offence, pet. My Pammy's as pretty as a picture.

Pam Herbert
(Coquettish) Oh, Stanley.

Stanley Herbert
It's true! Do you know, she's as beautiful as the day I married her, and I'll tell you for why. Every time a bit of her starts to drop, we whip her into surgery for an uplift!

Pam Herbert
Stanley's right!

Stanley Herbert
Oh yes, the surgeon's knife has had the lot of her! Face, stomach, thighs, bum ...

Pam Herbert
And I've had me titties done – good aren't they!

Stanley Herbert
I like 'em! Oh yes, I'm a self-made man, and she's my man-made wife!

Pam Herbert
That's one of Stanley's little sayings, that is!

Stanley Herbert
How long are you here for then, young couple?

Mrs Parker
Just a week.

Pam Herbert
All they could afford, Stanley.

Stanley Herbert
Oh well, never mind! We'll look after you for a week – eh! That's good of us isn't it! Cause for a celebration, that! Pedro, you lazy oaf! Get your big bum over here!

(Pedro the waiter appears.)

Pedro
Yes, Mr Herbert?

Stanley Herbert
Two champagne cocktails, sport! And two glasses of Sangria for our friends here. And none of your usual ambling! Chop chop!!

Pam Herbert
Pedro thinks Stanley's a character! Don't you, Pedro?

Pedro
(Drily) Indeed, Mrs Herbert.

(Mr Parker and Pedro speak in Spanish.)

Mr Parker
Sangria no gracias, solo un par de cervezas.

Pedro
Si Señor, gracias

Stanley Herbert
No no no! You don't have to speak the lingo! Oh no! The only lingo these people understand is the language of money!

Pam Herbert
D'you know, Stanley and I have been coming here for fifteen years and we pride ourselves on never speaking a word of Spanish!

(Pedro returns with drinks.)

Stanley Herbert
Eh! I said pronto, not half an hour, you dozy dago!

Pedro
Ha ha! Mr Herbert, you are a real character!

(He puts drinks down.)

Pedro
Aquí tienen las cervezas.

SUBTITLE:
'Here are your beers.'

Mrs Parker
Gracias, señor!

Pedro
Aquí tienen las cocteles de champán.

SUBTITLE:
'And here are your Champagne cocktails.'

Pedro
En los que me he orinado antes.

SUBTITLE:
'... which I urinated in earlier.'

Mr Parker
(Delighted) Gracias, señor!

Stanley Herbert
Cheers! *(Drinks)*

first met Paul in 1980, when I'd got a job in London during the university summer holidays, but had nowhere to live. I knew of Paul from an old school friend, Dave Cummings, and had met his girlfriend a couple of times. Being eighteen years old and naïve, I simply went round to Paul and his girlfriend's flat and asked if I could stay there for eight weeks. Flummoxed by my directness, they said yes, so I spent the next two months sleeping on their living-room floor. Both Paul and Mary, his then girlfriend, could not have been nicer to this stupid boy. Paul, who worked for Hackney council at the time, was as funny and as warm as I had heard, and I kept in touch with them for my remaining time at university, before plonking myself on their floor again, uninvited, when I left university in 1982. What are young people like? I guess I hero-worshipped Paul, three years my elder, and Mary, and assumed they'd love me living on their floor as much as I loved them looking after me, but after a couple of days they summoned up the courage to sit me down and tell me that perhaps I ought to find myself somewhere to live, to which I replied,

'Yeah yeah,' and carried on watching *Dallas*. So after a week or so, Paul would come in from work to find me and my friends spilling food all over his living-room carpet, and had to resort to subtle hints like 'Are you still ****ing here?' before storming out and slamming the door. After about three weeks, Harry the thick-skinned moron left Paul and Mary's flat to live round the corner, but I saw Paul at least twice a week at our local pub for the next four years. He was the funniest person I knew, and did the best impression of Adam Athanassiou, our local kebab shop owner – my less good impression of Adam eventually became Stavros. By the time I left Hackney, I was already doing *Spitting Image* and Stavros on *Saturday Night Live.* I had asked Paul to write for me, but he had never taken me seriously. Paul is warm, friendly and very intelligent. Everyone who works on my show will tell you that I'm the grumpy one and he is the life and soul. When I sit tearing my hair out over a script, Paul will humour me and be patient. When I'm pompous, he'll mercilessly put me down. He is the perfect professional partner for a moody old git like me.

Paul Whitehouse

DE DUTCH COPPERSH

The Dutch Coppers could be characters on *The Fast Show*. Paul has been doing his brilliant Dutch accent for years and I've always wanted to be able to use it somewhere. We tried Paul's Dutchman before a couple of years ago, as a young tourist with his Russian friend (me) who liked 'guitar-based rock – wow! It is sho goot!'. The characters got a mixed response from the studio audience, so we never did them again. With the Dutch Coppers, it just seemed terribly funny to me that, Holland being such a liberal country, they would talk, in the matter-of-fact way that policemen speak around the globe, about being dope-smoking, hippie-loving homosexuals. I was also concerned that my Russian had been the cause of the failure of our previous attempt to launch Paul's Dutchman, so this time I made sure I kept my gob shut and let Paul do his stuff without my less accomplished interference (though when I watch the Dutch Coppers now, I'm mortified to see how much face-pulling and eye-twinkling I do in the background. Why can't I resist trying to hog the limelight from Paul? I must be deeply psychologically disturbed. Hmmm ...).

Dutch Copper and partner in car.

Stephan
Hullo there. It's me, Captain Stephan Van der Haastgradgst of the Amsterdam police again, with my partner and also, I'm happy to say, my lover, Ronold.

(Ronold gives a wave.)

Stephan
Today we are called out to the PrinzenranzenFonzenVerhoffenstal Van Der Bik Memorial Park where there is some trouble because many people from the gay community are coming down there and are openly making love with no clothes on, and some old people who are using the park for walking their dogs are complaining, um. Obviously here in Amsterdam we can't tolerate this kind of behaviour, from the, er, old people, so we are explaining to them how beautiful the love can be between two people of the same sex, and we are encouraging the old people to form a semi-circle round the gay lovemakers, and they are clapping along and having an uplifting experience. Evening all.

The Self-righteous Brothers

I got the idea for Frank and George from this horrible old neighbour I used to have when I first got famous. He was small, and like a lot of small men, what he lacked in size he made up for in volume. He insisted on calling me 'Enfield' rather than Harry, and would invite himself round to give me his sage opinions on my work. 'Saw your show last night, Enfield. Made me smile in places, but you can drop them DJs for a start.' I'd nod 'hmmm' politely while thinking, 'As if I care a monkey's what you think, Ken.' Soon after I moved in, I had the builders in for a bit. To give him his due, Ken was very patient about the noise, but

at the end of each day he'd wait until the builders had gone, when he'd come round to look at what they'd done and say how terrible their workmanship was compared to his (he was an ex-builder). 'Oi, Enfield, come 'ere, son! Look at that joint there!' he'd say, pointing at a corner where new skirting board had been laid.

'It looks fine to me, Ken.'

'Yer jokin', aren't you, Enfield? Look! He should have dovetailed that! He'll have to rip the lot out and start again! How'd you let him get away with that?' he'd continue.

'Honestly, Ken, it's fine.'

'Fine!' He'd start to get angry, pointing his finger at me and yelling, 'You ever heard of quality of workmanship? I would never, EVER, have done sloppy work like that!' Here he was, in my house, shouting at me about something I was perfectly happy with and had nothing to do with him at all! The only thing that would calm him down was if I said, 'You're right, Ken – if only I'd got you to do the work,' whereupon he'd heartily agree and go into a long ramble about what a good job he would have done, how he wouldn't have let me choose the carpets I'd chosen, or paint the walls the colours I like, but *he* would have done it all *his* way and it would all have been much, much better. 'Oh, I'd 've done it for *you*, Enfield, yes. I wouldn't work for your mate Elton, though, naah! He's scum.' Poor Ben Elton! When I told him that if he ever bought a house my mad neighbour wouldn't do it up for him, you can imagine how heartbroken he was! Ken obviously had a terrible inferiority complex. Deep down in his brain he must have thought that he was horrible and that unless he spent his whole time boasting, everyone would hate him. I felt rather sorry for him. He really was a nutcase.

As soon as I had safely moved out of the flat and away from Ken for ever, I thought I must do him on telly. I started to think of his thoughts on Ben Elton in terms of a sketch: 'If Elton was to buy an 'ouse, which required refurbishment, and he come and begged me to do the work for him, I'd say, "No Elton, not for you. I'd do it for Enfield, but you're scum. Hoppit, son!"' I wanted to do the character with Paul, so I created two 'Kens' who attempted to prove how great they were to each other by saying how they'd slap about celebrities who mucked them about. The only time they didn't feel inadequate was when they were in their own little fantasy world. Just like poor, lonely, old Ken. I don't think he was ever happier than when he was yelling at me, after which he'd go down the pub and boast to his mates about putting me in my place. I loved the way Ken never called me anything but 'Enfield' or 'son', as if to say 'You may be a jumped-up celebrity but to me you're just "Enfield", 'cos I'm as good as you!' – as if I'd ever said he wasn't! So Paul and I decided that our characters, Frank and George, would only ever refer to celebrities by their surnames. The choice we made was based on celebrities who are always known by their Christian names and surnames, because they sounded better than those who are known by their surnames. We all often refer to sportsmen, for instance, using only their surnames: Cantona, Shearer, Wright, Beckham. This is because we're used to sports commentators doing the same. We generally refer to showbiz people by both names and it sounds odd just using the surname. Hence 'Gascoigne' is a footballer, but 'Bamber Gascoigne' used to present *University Challenge*; 'Hislop' is a goalkeeper, 'Ian Hislop' is on *Have I Got News For You*. 'I like the music of Elton John,' we say, but Frank and George say, 'I enjoy the music of John.' With Rowan Atkinson we say, 'Rowan Atkinson is so funny.' They say, 'I'll tell you who makes me smile – Atkinson.' When we did The Self-righteous Brothers for the first time, the audience cottoned on immediately. Here's that first sketch.

> Oh, I'd 've done it for you, Enfield, yes. I wouldn't work for your mate Elton, though, naah! He's scum

The Self-righteous Brothers on Edmonds

Int. Pub.

Frank (Harry)
No, in the world of light entertainment there are only three contenders for the crown: Barrymore, Forsyth, and of course Edmonds.

George (Paul)
Oh, Edmonds stands apart – I love his work. In my opinion, *The House Party* is a thing of genius at which laughter is compulsory.

Frank
He certainly is a comical nutcase.

George
Oh yes. You have to laugh at Edmonds.

Frank
You do, I caught my son *not* laughing at him the other day. I give him a slap.

George
Quite right, Frank. The antics of Crinkly Bottom call for compulsory mirth.

Frank
They certainly do. Mind you, much as I admire his work, if Edmonds come down our pub for a lunchtime drinking session, had a few too many, come into the family room, where I'm sitting enjoying my Guinness with the wife enjoying a lime cordial and the kiddie enjoying a Coke, if Edmonds come in pissed up and started using blue language in front of my wife and my kid ...

George
You'd be up there like a shot, Frank.

Frank
I'd be up there like a shot, George. 'Oi! Edmonds! No! I admire your uncanny ability to tickle the nation's Saturday evening funny bone, but I do not admire your blue language in front of my wife and kid.' I'd give 'im a slap! 'Out of the pub! Edmonds, you get yourself back to Crinkly Bottom and wash your mouth out with soap and water!'

George
Quite right, Frank. We can't allow our popular weekend entertainers to act like hooligans.

Frank
We can't afford it as a nation.

George
I mean, I admire Black.

Frank
Oh Black's the consummate entertainer.

George
No one can put a contestant at ease like Black does on *Blind Date*, and she'd be welcome to walk down my road any time she liked. But if she lobbed a brick through my front window ...

Frank
Ah no!

George
'Oi! Black! No! This is not a welcome surprise surprise. I admire your ability to reunite adopted twins after forty years apart and your superb singing voice, but that is not an excuse for vandalism, you deranged

ginger bitch.'

Frank
You'd have right on your side, George. I mean, it's not just these mindless acts of vandalism, is it?

George
If only it was, Frank.

Frank
It's the petty annoyances these major celebrities might get up to. I mean if Houston ...

George
Lovely girl, triffic singing voice.

Frank
Sure, sure. But if Houston walked up and down outside my house, trailing an ice lollypop stick up and down the railings – ting! Ting! Ting! Ting! Ting! Ting! Ting! All right, if she only did it once, but if she did it for an hour! While I'm trying to watch Sky Sport!

George
You'd be out there.

Frank
'Oi! Houston! No! I will not always love you if you carry on with that cacophony. Now 'oppit!'

George
And you'd be well in order there, Frank!

Frank
I tell you, if that Lee Travis so much as thought about nicking the lead off my roof I'd be down his farm straight away to kill 'is ducks ...

George
Bastards. These celebrities make you sick.

Frank
Scum.

(They sip drinks.)

'Good evening, ladies and gentlemen, and what a very pleasant evening it is!'
'It is indeed, and it's made even more pleasant by having such a splendidly pleasant audience.'

The Title

As you will guess from Mr Chomondley-Warner, I like old-fashioned things. The title sequence for a show is very important – it sets up the flavour of what is to come. When I started working on *Harry Enfield's Television Programme,* there had been lots of sketch shows around with very 'modern' title music and graphics – *The Lenny Henry Show*, *Rory Bremner, Naked Video* to name but three. I wanted my show to have the feel of a traditional family comedy show, so I wanted the titles to be simple, a bit silly – a pastiche of old-fashioned shows like Harry Worth or Mike Yarwood. I started with the music. I took the soldiers' chorus from Guiseppe Verdi's opera *Il Trovatore* and asked Kate St John, the classically trained multi-instrumentalist, formerly of the Dream Academy and Van Morrison, and now a performer in her own right, to do an 'Anglicized' arrangement of the piece. She did this expertly and made the Italian music into a very English, slightly pompous-sounding tune.

To this I added the visuals of 'The Real Me'. In the seventies, when Mike Yarwood was at the height of his career, the show in which he would perform his many impressions would always end with a song from Yarwood as himself – 'And this is the real me'. If my show was to involve me playing many different characters, I wanted to introduce it as 'The Real Me' – although, unlike Yarwood, I didn't want 'The Real Me' to be the real me. I wanted my television Real Me to be Mr Frightfully Pleased With Himself Old-fashioned Showbiz Star. A man with a 'Good news! I'm here!' idiot look in his eyes, and the self-satisfied smirk of One Who Knows He Is Great on his face. One of the things I'm most often asked to do by people who stop me in the street is my special smirk. I also do it to my wife when I'm right and she's wrong, until she hits me. The smirk came from my Dusty and Dick days on the London cabaret circuit. There were many rough venues where the audience would bottle you off in seconds if they didn't like you. My partner Bryan Elsley and I had a technique for getting the Millwall nutters to like us – that was to start our act in our plummiest accents:

'Good evening, ladies and gentlemen, and what a very pleasant evening it is!'

'It is indeed, and it's made even more pleasant by having such a splendidly pleasant audience.'

'It most certainly is.'

We would then both give ingratiating smirks to the audience, almost dribbling on the front rows, until they were all chuckling. Often, for added effect, I'd take the hand of someone like a tattooed biker girl in the front row and kiss it as if she were the Queen, leaving a large pool of slobber on the unfortunate recipient's limb. All this went down well with the nutters, who then allowed us to proceed with our act without interruption from their flying glasses.

So that's how the smirk came about. When Paul and Kathy joined the titles for *Harry Enfield and Chums*, we took the smirk a stage further, pretending to be the cast of a play wallowing in the applause of an ecstatic crowd at the post-show curtain call. I've always found curtain calls embarrassing when I've had to do them. They're embarrassing to watch too. I've seen many a duff play at the National Theatre, after which the hammy cast prances around, bowing and smirking for far too long, and we thoroughly enjoy sending them up.

Sequences

From the reaction I get in the streets, Tim is one of my most popular characters, along with the Slobs and Kevin. He was created by *Have I Got News for You*'s Ian Hislop and the cartoonist Nick Newman. When I worked on *Spitting Image,* Ian and Nick wrote the best sketches, so when I was looking for extra writers for my first series, they seemed an obvious choice. I went to see them at Ian's *Private Eye* office and they suggested various new characters, but the one I liked best was their idea for a posh, thick ex-public schoolboy. But to make him original, we all agreed, he couldn't just be stupid – he had to be terribly nice as well.

At the time I had a girlfriend whose friends all seemed to go out with posh City types called Tim who lived in Wandsworth, South London. Sometimes we'd have to go over there to parties, and in these conservative social circles the women would all go off into a gaggle and have a laugh and a chat, and I'd get stuck with their blokes. They were all extremely nice, but sadly we had absolutely nothing in common. Being incredibly well brought up, though, they'd do their best to try to make me fit in. 'Hi! Tim!' they'd say, giving me a firm handshake.

'Harry, hi,' I'd reply.

'Excellent to meet you, excellent! You in the City, Harry?'

'Um, no, I'm not, no.' A look of surprise and puzzlement would come over Tim's face. Not in the City? How unusual!

'What's your line, Harry?'

'Well, I'm, um, a comedian.' I hate saying I'm a comedian, it sounds such a silly thing to be.

'Right! ... Um ... Must be jolly funny being a comedian – ha!'

'Ha!' I'd say politely, 'Sometimes. Other times it's just work.'

'Right, OK, absolutely ... Um ... Where do you do this comedy?'

'Well, on telly, mainly.'

'Ah, excellent ... um ... have we seen you in anything?'

'Um, I did a thing called *Friday Night Live* on Channel Four, but I shouldn't think you've seen it.' I knew he wouldn't have done – posh people don't watch telly on Friday night.

'Right, um, excellent! Have you seen *Blackadder*? It really is excellent! Baldrick's an absolute total ninny. It really is a hoot!'

'What do you do, Tim?' Tim puts on his serious face.

'I'm in futures, yah.'

'How is the future looking?'

'Excellent, yah! Market's really buoyant at the mo' – um.'

'Good.' A deafening silence would follow for a few seconds. I'd rack my brain for something to say, but good old Tim would come to the rescue.

'D'you play rugger?'

'No, Tim, I'm afraid not.'

'OK ... Um ... Do you sail? We're going to the Isle of Wight next weekend – should be bloody good fun, you're more than welcome to come.'

'Thanks, but I don't sail.'

'OK, fine. How about golf? We're teeing off at 10.45 tomorrow morning, if you fancy a round?'

'Thanks, Tim. I don't play golf.'

'Probably wise, yup ... Excellent drop of wine this – do you follow the wine world, Harry?...'

Poor Tim, I could have been from a different planet. He made all the effort in the chat, and even though he must have found it as much hard work as I did, he *still* invited me to join him in just about everything he was doing. I always felt I

Tim Nice

could probably have said to the many Tims I met, 'I don't play golf or rugger and I don't sail, but I wouldn't mind snogging your girlfriend,' and they'd have replied, 'Right! Absolutely! Sure! Be my guest. She's a bloody good snog, as a matter of fact. Totally first-rate. Tremendous!'

The Tims were all jolly nice blokes, but Ian, Nick and I are not, so we decided to repay their generosity of spirit by ruthlessly taking the piss out of them. Tim Nice But Dim was born.

A look of surprise and puzzlement would come over Tim's face. Not in the City? How unusual!

But Dim

Tim's Lucky Break

Tim's flat in Fulham. There is a dining table set up in the living room with Charlie, his girlfriend Camilla, her friend Emma, Quintin and Phillippa as dinner party guests.

Charlie
You've got to see it, Emma. It's really, really funny. There's blood everywhere. There's a bit where this johnny gets his ear sliced off that's a scream. There was a girlie in front of us who honked into her popcorn.

(They all laugh.)

Tim
(Out of shot) Charlie!

(Charlie runs into kitchen. We see Tim spraying blackened dish with fire extinguisher.)

Tim
Sorry, burnt the taramasalata.

Charlie
Let's go straight to the main course. What's on the blackboard?

Tim
Ah! A bit of a speciality of mine, actually. Spag Bol à la Timbo.

Charlie
And what's that when it's at home?

Tim
Well, actually, it's um, fish fingers. I was doing the Spag Bol, when I remembered that I'd forgotten a couple of the ingredients.

Charlie
Which ones?

Tim
The Spag and the Bol.

Charlie
Ah!

Tim
Sorry, Charlie. Just a bit nervous – trying to impress Emma. Bloody nice girl, isn't she?

Charlie
Tim, you daft bugger – forget the crapola cooking. Totty's not impressed with all that new man bollocks. The way to totty's heart is through your wallet.

Tim
Ah. There's the trouble. I'm a bit stony at the moment since I've lost me job at Sotheby's. Yah, bit of a crossed line during a telephone auction. Flogged a Renoir to a minicab firm for £11.50. Unfortunate that, yah.

(Charlie looks at him with an idea dawning.)

Charlie
Look, Tim. As an old mate I can let you take over my slice of some pretty tasty action.

Tim
Really?

Charlie
Mmm. There's no cash up front, you just stump up some collateral against a pretty minimal liability risk. Do you understand?

Tim
No.

Charlie
Good. You just sign here and the cash will start flowing quicker than a vindaloo after ten pints of wallop.

Tim
I'm not just signing anything, Charlie.

Charlie
It's a napkin.

Tim
Oh, right, that's OK, then.

(Tim signs. They shake hands.)

Charlie
I'll fill in the rest later. You can go and tell Emma that you are seriously loaded. Congratulations. You're now officially a name at Lloyd's.

(Tim and Charlie go into dinner party holding two Champagne bottles each.)

Charlie
Grub's off everyone – let's get stinkoed.

All
Hurrah!

Tim
Thought we'd stick to the old Champers tonight, as I'm celebrating being pretty seriously loaded at the moment.

(Emma begins to show interest.)

Emma
How marvellous! Sit down next to me and tell me all about it.

Tim
(Embarrassed) Crikey! Harrr ... Harrr *(Snorts)* ... er, I ...

(Tim makes thumbs-up sign to Charlie.

Cut to the next morning. Tim is still dressed but looks dishevelled. His flat has been smashed up. Enter cleaning woman.)

Tim
Good morning, Mrs P. Sorry about the mess. Still, bloody good night last night. We played Charades. Charlie did *Robocop* 1, 2 and 3. You might like to start on the bathroom. You'll find it in there in the kitchen.

(Mrs P. goes next door.)

Tim
(Opening letter) What's this? Bumf from Charlie about Lloyd's. *(Reads)* 'Dear Tim. Good luck with Lloyd's. You are henceforth a member of the following syndicates: "BigQuake", "Tidewave", and "Oil Spill".' Good old Charlie! Real mate!

(Tim picks up paper. The headlines say 'Big Earthquake', 'Tidal wave', 'Massive Oil Spill'.)

Tim
OH, NO! *(Pause)* Major chiz, Mrs P. England are 181 for 5.

(Phone goes in goldfish bowl. Tim picks out receiver and answers it.)

Tim
Hullo? Crikey, that's quick! Blimey! Yah! I'll be right over, thanks very much.

(Tim puts down phone.)

Tim
You won't believe it, Mrs P., I joined Lloyd's last night and already there's five million owing. I'm off to collect my winnings.

(Mrs P. comes back in holding ripped-out bathroom sink.

Cut to ext. Street. Tim driving. Music.)

Tim
Ah, good, a parking space.

(Crash.)

Tim
Pity there was someone in it.

(Cut to ext. Shot of Lloyd's. Tim walking up steps.)

Tim
(Voice over) Hullo, Dobson! I haven't seen you since you were expelled for robbing the tuck-shop at penknifepoint.

(Cut to int. Lloyd's office.)

Lloyd's Official
Ah. Nice But Dim. Come in.

Tim
Head prefect! How was borstal?

Official
Don't be silly, Nice But Dim. That was a very long time ago.

(There are graphs all over wall going drastically downwards.)

Official
Now, you received a telephone call from us this morning saying that you owe us five million quid.

Tim
I owe you five million pounds?

Official
Yes, that's right, Nice But Dim. We're going to have to take your credit cards, your bank account, your building society account, your car and your house ...

Tim
Yikes.

Official
And your parents' house, and their parents' houses.

Tim
Anything else?

Official
Empty your pockets, would you?

(Tim begins to go through his pockets, pulling out the contents.)

Tim
Colouring-in pens ... Swiss army penknife ...

Official
Put it on the table.

Tim
Oh no, you can't have this – it's essential equipment for getting Champagne corks out of chaps' eyes!

Official
Hand it over!

Tim
I think that's absolutely outrageous!

(He puts it on table. Official looks at computer screen.)

Official
Now your credit card company says you bought something at a jeweller's this morning?

Tim
(Quivering lip) Yah, bit of a diamond engagement ring for my fiancée, Emma.

Official
(Puts out his hand) Thank you.

Tim
(Close to tears) Bloody nice ring, isn't it?

(Offical pockets the ring. He types into machine.)

Official
The engagement's off anyway. I'm afraid your credit rating no longer matches her requirements.

Tim
(Destroyed) Well that's it then. You've cleaned me out.

Official
Mmm?

(Cut to ext. Underpass. Two tramps are sitting on the ground. One of them is Tim. The other is trying to sell him a new home.)

Tramp
'Tis a grand, fine box, sir. A lot of inquiries about this one.

Tim
Well, I must admit, it is a bloody fine box. A bit small though, isn't it?

Tramp
Ah, but look! 'Tis a beautiful use of space. Ah, very suitable for a first-time buyer! And you see, it gets the light the whole day! Do you see what I mean now, you gullible twat?

Tim
Yah, I certainly do. I'll buy it.

Tramp
Good! Ah, it's a wise choice, sir. An excellent location, spitting distance of the City and all that.

(A gobbit of spit lands on Tim from a height.)

Charlie
Get a job, you bloody scrounger, before I have you arrested for ... harassment.

Tim
Charlie! Champion gob! Knew it had to be you!

Charlie
Nice But Dim? What on earth happened to you?

Tim
Lloyd's.

Charlie
Oh, you bloody idiot! You should've got out before it got too late. I saw the whole thing coming! Dumped all my liabilities on some unsuspecting ... idiot.

Tim
Blimey. Wish I'd thought of that, Charlie. Wish I had your brains.

Charlie
Yes, well that's all very interesting. I've got to get on and pork Emma. Oh dear, it's starting to rain. Give me your cardboard box, I don't want to get my brolly wet. Bye!

(Cut to Tim on ledge of Lloyd's building, about to jump.)

Tim
Ah well, cheerio, world!

(He jumps. Reveal he jumped from a ground-floor window.)

Bish. Never did have much of a head for heights. Hullo, Head Prefect.

Lloyd's Official
Shut up, Nice But Dim and listen. Now Lloyd's has taken a lot of flak recently and we've got to show the world that we're willing to put our house in order. Which is why we want you to head up our internal fraud inquiry.

Tim
I don't follow you.

Official
That's precisely what we had in mind. We would clear all your debts, give you an enormous salary, and throw in this.

(He holds up Swiss army penknife.

Cut to kitchen. Night. Dinner party. Charlie is crouched in agony. Tim is extracting Champagne cork from his eye with Swiss army knife.)

Charlie
Careful, you half-wit!

Tim
Attaboy Charlie!

Charlie
So you've been head of this inquiry for nine months. Have you found anything?

Tim
Not yet, no. But I'll let you into a secret in confidence. This week, I came damn near to finding my office.

Emma
(Out of shot) Charlie! Charlie! Come here at once!

Tim
God, I envy you, Charlie.

Charlie
(Hassled) Coming, darling.

(Charlie exits.)

Tim
Good old Emma. What a throughly bloody gorgeously lovely young totty.

Taxi-drivers often ask Paul Whitehouse, 'What's Harry like in real life?' or me, 'What's Paul like?' But with Kathy they always answer their own question: 'What's she like? I bet she's LUVVERLY, in't she? Aw, she's triffic she is! I bet she's got an 'eart of gold!' The truth is, she is triffic and luvverly and she has indeed got an 'eart of gold, and she manages to convey this in every character she plays. Kathy is not only a comedienne, she's an award-winning playwright and an actress. A good actor is generally better at comedy than a comedian.

Paul and I write the bulk of the material for my show, and with any luck, when we perform our scripts, they are as funny as when we first wrote them, but frequently they are not. But Kathy makes our scripts far funnier than we imagined they could be. She is frequently accusing me of 'giving her all the work' and it's generally true – I prefer writing for her than for myself. I do stereotypes, she acts.

Wayne and Waynetta Slob started as a stereotype lumpenproletarian couple who ate and smoked too much. I thought they might last one series, if we were lucky. But then we cast Kathy and immediately she gave our stereotype an extra dimension. She didn't 'ham up' her performance, as I, like most comics, am inclined to do. As a serious actress she performed her role seriously. She gave the stereotype we'd written humanity. Waynetta became much nicer than we'd imagined and our scripts improved accordingly. In the first series we wrote slapstick shouting matches: 'Waynetta! Look! I've got us a new car.' 'I don't like it.' 'Ay?' 'It's brown.' 'So what?' 'It is a brown car.' 'I know it's a brown car, brown is a frightfully smart colour for a car, you daft slag.' 'I DON'T LIKE BROWN!' 'WHAT'S WRONG WITH BROWN?' 'IT'S BROWN! BROWN IS BROWN! THAT'S WHAT'S WRONG WITH BROWN!' But by the third series, Kathy had transformed her character, and I had mimicked her transformation. Wayne and Waynetta had become Britain's best loved underdogs.

I love Waynetta, I love Perry, I love Kathy. I have no doubts about her enormous contribution to my own success. I hope to continue working with her for many years to come.

Kathy Burke

The Lovely Wobbly Randy Old Ladies

For some reason, I've always been popular with old women. Aged seventeen, I was a milkman in my school holidays and used to be invited in for coffee by quite a few old ladies who would frighten the living daylights out of me with their flirting. 'Ooh, you've eyes to die for, Milkman!' 'Ooh, if I could go back to my youth, I'd 'ave you for breakfast.' The nearest I got to an actual proposition was from one naughty old dear who, although she'd grown into the body of a 75-year-old, had the twinkly eyes of an eighteen-year-old and, 'I may be a mangy old cat but that don't mean I wouldn't lap up your cream! Way hey!' As I sped for the door, she let out a wicked cackle, bless her. Having done the whinging old Gits, I thought I'd have a go at doing the opposite – happy old girls – and what better role-models than those lovely, wobbly, randy, old ladies from my milkman days. I remembered an old friend of mine who used to mimic her mum by going, 'Ooh! Young Man!'. I decided to try this as the catch phrase, and it worked!

The Lovely Wobbly Randy Old Ladies are great fun to do – but hot work. TV studios are hot enough with all the lights beaming down on you, but with a ton of wobbly padding on as well Kathy and I sweat buckets. The padded costumes can't be washed, or they lose their shape, so between series the sweat-soaked stuff is left to fester in a store room. When we put them on now, as well as sweating, we stink to high heaven!

The Lovely Wobbly Randy

and the Gas Man

Hild (Kathy)
Have I missed him?

Glad (Harry)
No. It's still that young girl doing the weather. Get off, you silly Moo! We want Mr Rotivator!

Hild
Here he is! Young man!

Glad
Young man!

Hild
Oooh, we think you're lovely, Mr Rotivator — you're like a lovely dark version of Arthur Askey.

Glad
I tell you what, Mr Rotivator — you can go through my undergrowth any time you like!

Hild
Young man! There may be snow on my roof but there's a roaring fire in me grate!

Glad
Ooh, if I was your age!

Hild
If you were our age!

Both
Young man!

(Doorbell.)

Glad
Ooh! There's the doorbell. That'll be the lovely young gas man! How do I look, Hild?

Hild
Gorgeous!

(Glad hurries to front door and opens it.)

Glad
Hello, young man!

(Glad ushers him in.)

Hild
Coo-ee!

Gas Man
Hello, ladies, have I come too early?

Glad
Ooh, young man!

Hild
Wash your mouth out with soap and water, you naughty young man!

Glad
Young man!

Hild
Where's the lovely dark boy that was here yesterday?

Gas Man
Er, he begged me to come today. Now where's the gas leak this time?

Glad
You're a lovely young man too, you know, young man! D'you know we think you're the spitting image of a young Lester Piggot!

Gas Man
If you could just show me where ...

Hild
Go on, show us your muscles.

Gas Man
If you could just show me where you smelt the gas, eh?

Old Ladies

Glad
Ooooh, you saucy devil. It's in the bedroom this time.

(Hild takes his hand.)

Hild
Follow us!

Gas Man
Ladies, you haven't got any appliances upstairs.

Hild
Ooooh, appliances! Did you hear that Glad? Appliances! ... Young man!

Glad
From Anne Summers! Young man!

Hild
Ooh! How could you say such a thing, you saucy monkey! At your age!

Glad
At our age!

Both
Young man!

Gas Man
Shall I just check over your

pipework then?

(Both sigh sexually.)

Hild
How could you say such a thing to a couple of old ladies?

Glad
Young man!

Gas Man
Look! If it's not your pipework, what have you got me round here for?

Hild
Ooh you are strict!

Glad
In the kitchen young man. The grill! It don't work!

Gas Man
Right, thank you!

(He moves towards door into kitchen. They bar his progress.)

Hild
So if you fancy a nice bit of crumpet – you'll just have to make do with us!

Glad
You can stick your poker between my muffins any time you like!

Hild
Ooh! How could you say such a thing?

Glad
There you go again! Young man!

Gas Man
Can I get through, please? Can I just get through?

Hild
No no no no no no ... First things first: we've made you a little snack.

(She holds up massive plate of fancy cakes and rolls.)

Glad
Tuck in, young man! Ooh, breathe in, Hild. Smell his lovely, sweaty, sweaty sweat!

Hild
Mmm and look at his lovely bulge. He's like a young Desert Orchid!

Gas Man
Look ... Ladies, please. How about, you two, just stay here, right ... I'll take my bag of t ... spanners, and go through ... into the kitchen ... and get on with my work.

Glad
Get on with the job up my back passage?

Hild
With all your tackle out?

Both
Young man!

Glad
Let's go for it, Hild?

Hild
Alright, Glad!

(They get him on the floor.)

Gas Man
Waargh!

Glad
You get his top off, I'll get his down belows!

Hild
Stop struggling, you naughty young gas man! You're obviously gagging for it!

Glad
Don't you just love being in control?

(Hild does thumbs-up sign.)

The Manager of a Football Team

Since I started doing my own show, my job has not only been to write and act, but also to have an 'overview' of the show as a whole. It's a bit like being a football team manager. Before my first series I had to 'pick a team' of characters to do which I thought would have a broad appeal across the country – the young and the old, the posh and the common, the family stereotypes and the mad idiots. I wanted the team to have something for everyone – so if you didn't like The Slobs you'd still watch for Tim Nice But Dim and Mr Chomondley-Warner. Or if you hated Tim you'd like the Old Gits. Plus I wanted a few 'substitutes' – one-off characters who would pop up once in a series but weren't part of the 'first team'.

When I'm making the shows, I have to believe that all the characters are brilliant – otherwise I don't perform them as well as I should – so it's only after a series is made and finally chopped together that I can allow myself to look critically at the characters and see which ones are working and which are not. Then, before next season it's time to give the characters that aren't working free transfers to obscurity, and to buy in fresh blood to give the team new life.

Kevin

The youngest creation for the first series of *Harry Enfield's Television Programme* was Kevin. Most families have a little boy like Kevin. Boys are generally stupider than girls. Girls have much more patience – they like drawing, painting, dressing up, doing creative things with their parents; boys like whizzing about and making a lot of noise, jumping on furniture and hurling themselves at walls. I made poor Kevin as hyperactive a little boy as I could, with an attention span of zero seconds, and gave him a big curly red wig which bounced up and down, accentuating his inability to keep still. As I am nearly six foot tall myself, Kevin was taller than the rest of his family, which helped to exaggerate the plight of my hapless relatives, as I jumped, squawked and gyrated around them until their patience snapped. I was the cuckoo in the nest.

The sketch I most enjoyed doing was 'Christmas Dinner', to which my granny came. When I was a small child myself, various old people used to come to lunch with my parents and frighten the life out of me with their strange smells of pipes and perfumes, their slow speech and false teeth. Kevin, having no conception of the word tact, could say everything I used to think as a child.

Like a lot of my characters, Kevin the little brother was incredibly irritating. It was always a difficult line to tread between him being funny and just plain annoying. In the second series of *Harry Enfield's Television Programme* we tried to transform him into a gawky, mumbling teenager who was totally unsure of his new, spot-covered, evil-smelling body, but it didn't seem to work – he was just too boring. So we 'lost' Kevin – he never appeared in my second series, and as far as I was concerned, he would never appear again.

Before my third series, I had a brainwave. I suddenly remembered how, during my own years as a teenager, the most abiding factor in my life was my hatred of my parents. It happened overnight. I went to my first party, snogged a girl and entered a new world. Before the party my parents had smiled and said, 'Have a good time,' and I'd replied, 'Thanks!' A few hours later, when I returned home, they asked, 'How was the party?' 'Cuh! OK!' I replied. As if they'd understand! These sad people with no idea about what life was *really* about! I now *knew* what life was about – snogging, girls, girls and, er, snogging – and here were these *old* people who liked reading and gardening looking at me with patronizing grins as if I was just a kid or something. I *hated* them.

For Kevin's 'birth' as a teenager we had him

As if they'd understand! These sad people with no idea about what life was really about. I now knew what life was about — snogging, girls, girls and, er, snogging

– from LITTLE BROTHER to TEENAGER

go straight from hyperactive little brother to parent-hater in the time it took for the clock to strike twelve on his thirteenth birthday. Straight away the audience got what I was up to. I've had so many letters from parents saying, 'Thank you! I thought my teenager was the only one like that!' I'm afraid not. Nearly all of us go through a 'Kevin' stage. There's nothing to be done about it!

My favourite Kevin sketch is 'Perry Goes to Manchester'. I love Perry. He's gawky, naïve and he hero-worships Kevin – which is *really* sad. This sketch was based on another of my teenage experiences, going to my first punk rock gig – the Sex Pistols, who were supporting Eddie and the Hot Rods in Guildford in 1976. There I was, a middle-class ex-public schoolboy who was now at the local school and was watching the Pistols with his new working-class mates. Within a week of the gig I'd chopped off my hair, got some jumble shop straight trousers and developed a mock cockney accent. Now my parents were worse than ever – middle-class ponces in their stupid country cottage – when I was a working-class punk who wanted to live in a tower block and have no future on the dole. I was probably a very stupid boy, but it was fun at the time. Anyway, this sketch is my experience brought up to date – with Oasis taking the place of the Pistols.

Perry Goes to
Manchester

Kevin on sofa. Mum in kitchen.

Mum
Perry's back from Manchester today, isn't he?

Kev
Mmmm.

Mum
That's nice. Have you missed him this week?

Kev
No!

Mum
I expect you're excited about seeing him, aren't you?

Kev
No!

(Mum ruffles his hair affectionately.)

Mum
You are a silly.

Kev
Get off, I hate you.

(She tuts and goes upstairs. Kev stares vacantly until the doorbell rouses him. He answers the door. Perry brushes past him walking in an Oasis-style way. Dressed in an Oasis-style way.)

Perry
(Mancunian accent) Alright, our Kev?

(Kev looks vaguely bemused.)

Kev
Alright, Pel? How was Manchester?

Perry
Result, sorted, top, mad for it.

(He takes a defiant swig of Tizer.)

Kev
Did you go to the Oasis gig?

Perry
Might have done. Who's asking?

Kev
Well ... me.

Perry
Oh right, yeah, sorted, our Kev.

Kev
Were they brilliant?

Perry
Yeah, sorted, you know, mad for it. I can't remember, I was so out of it.

(Does a bit of air punching.)

Kev
How was your aunty?

Perry
That 'has been', I dunno. Who cares? You know, our Kev, the way I look at it is there's two types of people, us and wankers.

(Kev is impressed by Perry's Northernness and attempts a Northern accent with hilarious results.)

Kev
Yeah. Right, our Perry. Sorted!

Perry
So how has dead town been

while I was away?

Kev
It's been a right bummer.

Perry
Chill out, our Kev, and get one on.

(Perry hands Kev a bottle of Tizer.)

Kev
Cheers, Perry, oh, I mean our Perry. Sorted! Yeah it's been a real boring week. Been in my room a lot listening to Oasis all week. I know all the words to the songs.

Perry
Uncool. Learning words is what you do at school.

Kev
Oh, yeah. Sorry, our Perry. I hate school, it's where they mess up your mind.

Perry
Spot on, our kid. Teachers teach you how to be stupid.

Kev
Yeah!

(Mrs Patterson comes in.)

Mum
Hello, Perry. Did you have a nice time in Manchester?

Perry
(Old polite self) Yes thank you, Mrs Patterson, please thank you –

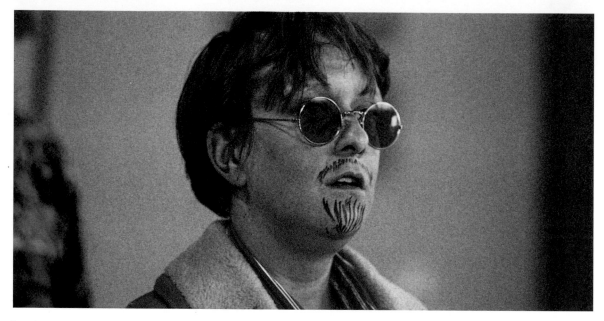

but it was very cold, ha ha ha!

Mum
Gosh you've got a little bit of a beard – how. grown up.

Perry
Thank you.

(She goes upstairs. Perry turns to Kev.)

Perry
She's alright, your mum. I'd like to shag her.

(He strides to front door. Kev goes after him.)

Kev
Ooh! Um, I'd like to shag your mum as well!

(Perry exits. Kev goes back into kitchen, nonchalantly says to Mum:)

Kev
Yeah, I'll 'av some bread 'n' drippin' for us teas, our mum.

Mum
Kevin, why are you talking in that extraordinary way?

Kev
Wot? Don't know wot tha' means.

Mum
I mean why are you and Perry pretending to be Northerners? You sound very silly.

Kev
Y' don't know nothing. I mean nowt! I'm real! You're jus living their lies! Huh!

(Strides off, turns.)

Kev
I hate yer!

Scousers

'd always wanted to do some Liverpudlians. Liverpool has always fascinated me, and being a Southern softie, I thought it would be a good idea to do something for Northern viewers. The Scousers were based on the early days of *Brookside,* where Barry and Terry were best of mates but always scrapping. So we came up with three silly boys, Ga', Ba' and Te', all with the curly hair of their *Brookside* models. I'd always thought I did a good Liverpool accent, but when we started doing the Scousers I realized my accent wasn't a patch on the real thing, supplied by Joe McGann and Gary Bleasdale. Often they'd correct my lousy accent in mid-recording. There's one sketch, in hospital, where I go, 'I've broken me eeem!' and Gary Bleasdale says, pointedly, 'I'll break your other *orm* if you're not careful.' Often, when we're recording in front of an audience, I'll say a line like 'Ay, weer shall we gao ferruzz holidees diz year den?' and the other two will be so appalled with my accent that instead of doing their next lines in the script they'll go, 'Yer wa'? Yer wa'? Yer wa'? Where d' 'ell do you come from, mate?' and after encouraging the studio audience to jeer and boo me to their heart's content, will make me do it again.

Probably the best catch phrase to come out of the Scousers was one not known to me when we first wrote them, but was introduced by Joe and Gary. That's 'Dey doo dough don't de dough?' ('They do though don't they though?'), although 'Alright! Alright! Calm down!' is the one I most get shouted at me when I'm up in Liverpool. After first doing the Scousers, I was a bit nervous of what Liverpudlians would think, but they've been really brilliant to me and seem to have taken us on as city symbols. Nothing pleased me more than turning on the football one day and seeing the camera panning round the Liverpool fans, in the middle of whom was a whole bunch of blokes in Scouser frizzy wigs and false moustaches – it was the highest praise.

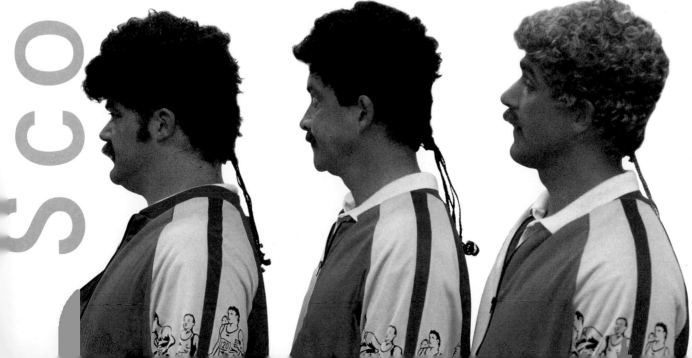

Scousers Wedding

All Asleep.

Gary: Calm down, calm down.

Terry: Eh, are you lookin' at me. Oh yeah, oh yeah.

Barry: Dey doo dough don't de dough?

(Waking up with phone ringing.)

Barry: Shut it, you. Are you telling me we're late? Oh Christ, we are. Com'on. We're late.

All: We're late, we're late.

Terry: Hey, are you telling me we're late?

Barry: Year, I friggin' am.

Terry and Gary: Eh, eh, eh.

Gary: Calm down, calm down. Did you just wake us up?

Barry: Yeh, I friggin' did.

Terry: Alright, calm down, calm down. Come ed, we're late.

Gary: We're late for what?

Terry: Are you asking me what you're late for?

Gary: Eh, eh.

Barry: Alright. Just calm down, calm down, calm down. What are we late for?

Terry: Well maybe if we remembered what we did last night.

Barry: I remember. We went to a stag night last night.

Terry: Oh yeah.

Gary: But whose stag night was it?

Terry: Oh it was that twat with the moustache.

Gary: Oh that's right. It was your stag night, Terry.

Terry: Are you calling me a twat with a moustache ... Oh Christ. I am!

All: Hang on ... Who are you marrying?

Terry: Oh you know, that pregnant bird ... What's her name ...

Gary: Oh I know ... 'Preggers'. Let's go.

Terry: Hey! Hang on, where's my best man?

Gary: I'm your best man.

Barry: I'm your best man.

Terry: Hang on, eh, eh ... Alright, alright. I'm the friggin' best man.

All: Eh, eh, eh.

(Later in church.)

Priest: Who is the best man?

Barry and Gary: We are.

Priest: I see. Can I have the ring please.

Barry and Gary: *(Fighting)* Eh, eh.

Barry: There you go, Father Terry off *Brookside.*

Priest: Terrald John George Paul Ringo Bleasdale Scouser, do you take this woman to be your wife?

(Baby cries.)

Barry: Shut it, you!

Priest: And do you, Sheila Preggers Boswald Beeshit Barnes Begnit Jenny Ferry Mersey Girobank Ticklesclit Grubber take this man to be your husband?

Terry: I never knew your name was Sheila.

Sheila: You never asked ... I do.

Priest: Terrald, do you solemnly swear to leave Liverpool at the earliest opportunity and live elsewhere and spend the rest of your life going on about how great Liverpool is without ever returning?

Terry: I do.

Barry: Oh he do doh doh di do.

Gary: Di do.

Priest: Do you swear to annoy everyone you meet by going on and on and on about the marvellous sense of humour Scousers have?

Terry: I do.

Priest: And then get drunk and hit the person that you're talking to?

Terry: I do.

Priest: Good. I now pronounce you Scouse and Scouse. You may give the bride a love bite.

Sheila: Eh!

Gary and Barry: Eh! Eh!

All: Eh! Eh! Eh!

(At the reception.)

Terry: Now, I'd like to call on the bride's bro to say a few words.

Bride's Bro: I know we'd all like to thank little Jimmy for taking the time off primary school and supplying us with the cars. It all seems very pleasant, although I don't know what they're gonna do with all them videos and thirty-two car radios. We'd also like to thank the fat bloke for sorting out the cake. Alright, fat bloke.

Fat Bloke: Alright, Brookie.

Gary: Would you look at him, that dirty git, he's a ... yes he is.

Terry: Oh, Gary, shut it will you.

Gary: Tell him to shut it with all his bloody pontificating. Come down here you dirty git. Come on, come on.

Terry: Shut up.

Bride's Bro: And will you all raise your glasses once again as the bridegroom's father wants to make a speech.

All: Go on, go on.

Terry: And now I'd like to call on my bros to make the best man's speech.

Gary: I'll never forget the time when our Terry shagged fifteen birds in a week and that calls for a clap.

Sheila: I never wanna see you again in my life.

Terry: Alright, love, see ya!

Barry: Ta ta, love, take care.

Terry: Marriage wasn't working anyway.

Bride's Bro: And now to the dance floor for the fight.

All: Yeah, yeah, yeah, eh eh, etc.

How the Series Gets Made

From the first day of writing to the first programme being shown on television usually takes about nine months. The process involved is as follows.

JANUARY TO APRIL: WRITING

A series of my show Is slx half hours, or three hours In total. For this, we will commission about six hours of material to be written and use the best half. The rest gets chucked away. Paul and I write about four hours of stuff, and usually end up using about two and a quarter. Our typical writing day will be as follows.

9.50 a.m.: I sit down at home with my computer and jot down ideas while I wait for Paul, who always promises to arrive at 10.00 on the dot.

10.20: Paul arrives, complaining that he couldn't find anywhere to park. He makes me make him a cup of coffee and tells me how he didn't sleep last night because Molly, his youngest daughter, has a cold. He then tells me how old and washed-up I am and reads me something unflattering about me from his newspaper. He then tells me how great he is and recites his latest brilliant creations from *The Fast Show*.

11.00: We finally start work. We discuss a character, say, Kevin, and think of situations for him until one makes us laugh. 'How about Kevin losing his virginity?' 'And turning normal!' 'Yes!' Then we're away. I generally sit at the computer tapping away while Paul fidgets and tries to tell me anecdotes, which I ignore, keeping my eyes glued to the keyboard. We shout lines at each other, and if they make us laugh, they go in. If I shout a line at Paul and he doesn't like it, he stares at me with a blank look as if I'm a weird pervert. I know then not to bother writing it down. If Paul tries one on me and I don't like it, I either pretend he isn't in the room or go 'hmmm' or 'perhaps', which he knows means 'definitely not'. Usually when I reject one of his jokes he comes up with another immediately, but occasionally he's more stubborn and will repeat the line, ending it with his Sid James cackle, 'Har Har Har!', to show me how wonderfully funny he thinks it is. I then scrunch up my face and say, 'Paul, no,' as if he was a silly little boy who knew if he dropped the glass it would smash, but dropped it anyway. Paul then bites his lip, rolls his eyes and folds his arms, as if to say: 'If you're going to be unreasonable, Harry, there's nothing I can do.' He then sulks until I roar with laughter at his next line, when all is forgiven.

1.30: Lunchtime. Go to the pub and talk shop. Paul will slag off some rival comic and I'll defend this person, acting superior and staying above such petty rivalries. Paul will then mention someone I don't like and I'll slag them off for a bit, until Paul tells me I'm a pathetic hypocrite.

2.00: Back to work. We'll read through what we wrote that morning and cut bits out that now seem not very funny. Then we'll write another sketch and then think about a couple of other ideas to write the next day. Sometimes we start to write a

Norm after 25 Gits 4F

sketch and then give up, because it doesn't seem to be going anywhere. Here's an example of one that never got finished.

Don't and the Spilt Egg

Don't's kitchen. Don't enters and sits at table. His wife is standing by the cooker.

Don't
Morning, The Wife! ONLY ME!! I'll have an egg this morning, please, The Wife, boiled for four and a half minutes or four point five minutes in metric terms. An egg boiled, a boiled egg is what I require, please, The Wife, thank you, ta. A boiled egg. Oh yes ... You don't wanna fry my egg! I don't want a fried egg! I want a boiled egg, The Wife! And if you were thinking of surprising me with an egg scrambled, think again, scrambled egg no! Neither scrambled or fried, and poach it not, for a boiled egg is what I want. Boiled egg. Yes! Yes! Yes! Yes! Yes! Yes! Yes! Yes! *(His wife is now a bundle of nerves. She drops the egg by mistake, it breaks on her arm, white goes on her sleeve, yolk on her leg and shell and rest on the floor.)* Now I do not believe you wanted to do that, did you, The Wife? You didn't want to do that! You've broken the egg. You didn't want to break the egg, did you? Did you? Did you? Did you? No! A boiled egg is what I required, not a broken one. Look! You don't wanna have albumen on your sleeve, yolk on your leg and shell on the floor! Albumen on your sleeve, yolk on your leg and shell on the floor is not what you want, is it? Is it? Is it? Is it? No!

At this point we were so bored of Don't and annoyed with the stupid prat, we gave up.

4.00: By now we're sick of the sight of each other and Paul leaves, promising to arrive on time at 10.00 a.m. on the dot the next day.

After about three months of this, we have enough scripts to more or less form a show. We then spend the next month getting all the scripts together, including those written by other people. We then chuck the worst away and rewrite the rest, as many times as we need to until we are happy with them. Usually we rewrite each of our own sketches about four times before we get to make them.

MAY: PRE-PRODUCTION

This is a planning stage. The first thing that gets decided is which bits need to be filmed outside, or with special effects, and which bits can be done in front of a studio audience. The whole of some sketches have to be filmed, for instance, 'Women! Know Your Limits!' or the Toddlers, where the BBC's biggest studio is totally overtaken with oversized sets.

Other sketches take place partly in the studio and partly on film. Take, for instance, 'Kevin Loses his Virginity'. The party where Kevin does the business was filmed at a house in South London. Then the next morning, when I come downstairs a new person, was filmed in front of an audience at the BBC, including me talking to Perry on the doorstep. But when I shut the door on Perry, we cut to stuff we filmed months before, as Perry kicks a can down the road outside Kevin's house.

During pre-production we prepare for three weeks of filming around London, getting together the film crew, hiring the other actors needed and going through the scripts one more time.

JUNE: THREE WEEKS' FILMING

Filming takes a long time. We try to film about five minutes of material a day. A typical filming day might be:

The first two days' editing are awful, as we look through everything we've just filmed and see me cock up my lines again and again and again, before I eventually get it right.

I've been really lucky with warm-ups. I had two brilliant blokes who both went on to far better things – Mark Lamarr and Lee Hurst.

Outside by Tower Bridge: Jurgen joins a group of tourists.

Inside an office by Tower Bridge: Wayne and Waynetta beat up a 'Sound Financial Adviser'.

Inside an aeroplane: Wayne and Waynetta eat too much.

In the jungle: Wayne and Waynetta after plane crash.

7.00: I get picked up from home.

7.30: I arrive at Tower Bridge and go into make-up, where Annie McKewan will transform my head into Jurgen's.

8.30: Into wardrobe, to put on Jurgen's clothes.

8.45: I'll meet with the director and discuss the day's shooting.

9.00: We film Jurgen at Tower Bridge, doing re-take after re-take because of all the noise from boats going past blowing their hooters and planes landing at Docklands airport.

11.00: We finish filming the sketch. The crew go and set up in an office and I change into Wayne, which takes an hour.

12.00: Kathy Burke and I go on set and film us with our 'Sound Financial Adviser'.

1.00: Lunch.

1.30: Kathy and I are driven to the BBC – still in costume. The sight of Wayne and Waynetta being chauffer-driven turns a few heads!

2.00: We rehearse our plane scene in a mocked-up Jumbo jet in a BBC studio.

3.00: We start filming the scene.

5.00: We finish filming the scene and move over to another set to rehearse us in front of a crashed plane.

6.00: We finish filming and go to clean up and get out of our smelly costumes.

6.30: We go home!

END OF JUNE: A WEEK'S EDITING

The first two days' editing are awful, as we look through everything we've just filmed and see me cock up my lines again and again and again, before I eventually get it right. There's also always lots of footage of me being bossy to Paul. For instance:

Director: OK, action!
Harry: Sorry, one sec. Paul, don't say 'Gold Standard', say 'Goowld Stennded'.
Paul: I'm gonna, H.
Harry: Well you didn't on the last take.
Paul: Yes I did, H.
Harry: No you didn't.
Paul: I flippin' did!
Director: He did actually, Harry.
Harry: Well, I didn't hear him.
Paul: You wanna listen, don't you.
Director: Can we do this please? Action!
Paul: Do you think the government should come off the Goowld Stennded?
Harry: Paul, don't say 'Gold Standard', say 'Goowld Stennded'.
Paul: I BLOODY WELL DID!!
Director: Cut!

After two days, all my bossiness, grumpiness and fluffed lines are on the cutting room floor and we spend the next three days chopping the bits of usable stuff into sketches. Three weeks' filming equals fifteen days, excluding weekends. So we should have 15 X 5 mins, or 75 minutes of sketches that can be shown to the studio audiences.

JULY AND AUGUST: SIX WEEKS' STUDIOS

On the Friday of each week we perform seven sketches to a studio audience, who have got free tickets for the show after answering an advert in *Time Out*, the London listings magazine. We rehearse from Monday till Thursday in Central London and then, having learnt our lines and moves, spend all Friday rehearsing at the BBC studio for the director and cameramen. Then in the evening, we do the show.

We are limited by time and space as to how much we can do in each studio show. Just like a play in a theatre, we have sets on the stage and an audience. The difference is that between the audience and actors are cameras to film us, and above the audience's heads are monitors for them to watch the filmed stuff we plat in to them and microphones to record their laughter. We only have room for five sets on the studio floor, so we can't run a studio show as it will eventually come out on TV. There are usually between eleven and thirteen sketches a programme, because there simply isn't enough room for all the sets. Also, because it takes such a long time for me to get changed and made up between characters, we have to 'double up' by doing two sketches with the same characters to one audience, preferably in the same set. So before we do the studios, we look at which characters and sketches will be most convenient to do each week.

Don't: BEFORE PRINT/BEER
SCENE 19/7/94.

A typical studio might look like this:

Sketch 1: Wayne and Waynetta win the Lottery.
Sketch 2: Perry comes round after seeing Oasis.
Sketch 3: Kevin pretends to be ill to skive off school.
Sketch 4: The Scousers go on holiday to Spain.
Sketch 5: Lee and Lance – 'Who's That Girl?'
Sketch 6: Lee and Lance – Lance's imaginary girlfriend.
Sketch 7: Tim goes to see the bank manager.

These sketches might eventually all appear in different TV programmes, but they make the best use of set space and time for make-up changes, if we do them like this. It takes three hours to do seven sketches, so it's a long haul for the audience, and for us. This is how an evening goes.

7.00: The audience arrives.

7.25: The warm-up man comes on and tries to warm everyone up with a few jokes. Poor warm-up man – everyone's come to see me, Paul and Kathy and no one wants to see him. He's always someone unknown and has to be brilliant to win the audience over. I've been really lucky with warm-ups. I had two brilliant blokes who both went on to far better things – Mark Lamarr and Lee Hurst.

7.30: I come on and do my own little warm-up. When I first appear in front of the audience, I introduce myself, Paul and Kathy, tell a few silly jokes, then tell the audience that if I fluff my lines they must hurl abuse at me. We then have a practice session where they all point at me and yell a word which I can't repeat in this family book, but it rhymes with oil tanker. After a couple of minutes of everyone yelling at me, we start the show.

7.35: Sketch 1 – Wayne and Waynetta win the Lottery. We play in film of Wayne and Waynetta buying their Lottery tickets, then move straight into live filming of us at home, winning the Lottery. Kathy hits me on the nose by mistake, which is agony, but the audience loves it. Kathy and I get giggly and instead of taking five minutes we take fifteen to get through the material. We have to do the second part of the sketch the next week, as we don't have room for the set of their posh new Lottery-funded home in the studio this week.

7.50–8.05: Kathy and I change to Perry and Kevin. While this is happening the audience is played in some of the stuff we filmed in the weeks before, on the monitors above their heads. Kathy and I have monitors in our dressing and make-up room, and as we are changing we can hear the audience's reaction to sketches. 'Women! Know Your Limits!' goes down well. The first Julio Geordio sketch comes on. They've never seen him before – how will he go down? They laugh a bit at the name, then at Paul talking in 'Spanish' and not understanding what I'm saying. The sketch ends – they've quite enjoyed it. We play them the second Julio Geordio sketch. They laugh less. They think it's going to be the same as the first, then they hear Paul go from 'Spanish' to broad Geordie and back again and WOOF! They love it! We play them two more Julios and they can't get enough. Now Mr Dead comes on. No laughter at all. Oh dear. They hate it! We play them six Mr Dead sketches and two get titters. Normally I'd chuck the lot in the bin after a reaction like that, but Paul, Kathy and I like Mr Dead, we want him in the TV show a bit, so we keep two sketches and the rest get chucked away.

8.10: Sketch 2 – Perry comes round after seeing Oasis. Kathy and I are finally dressed and made up as Perry and Kevin. After all the Mr Deads the audience are as Mr Dead as dodos themselves when I come out, but Kathy's entrance as Perry trying to be like Liam of Oasis goes down a storm – we're up and running again. The sketch takes about five minutes to film, and then another ten for re-takes, where cameramen missed their shots, or I fluffed my lines. Kathy has to do her 'Liam' entrance again too, as the first time she did it the audience didn't stop laughing or clapping for two minutes, which would look boring on TV, so we tell them not to clap for more than ten seconds this time.

8.25: Sketch 3 – Kevin pretends to be ill to skive off school. This sketch goes well, but not as well as the last as Kathy isn't in it.

8.30: I go to change into a Scouser. As I change, I hear the audience's reaction to more film stuff we're showing them. Tory Boy at the Tory Conference goes well – last week no one laughed very much at it. Audiences are funny like that – you show them exactly the same thing two weeks running and get totally different reactions.

8.45: Sketch 4 – The Scousers go on holiday to Spain. We have to do this round the back of the studio, as there isn't enough space for the set round the front. The cameras are fed through the monitors so the audience can see what's happening. It's never as good being 'round the back', but Mark and Gary are on top form and the sketch goes fine.

8.55: I'm off to change again, into Lee. We play in more stuff – 'Women! Don't Drive!' and 'L is for Labour. L is for Lice' go well, a sketch called 'Bird in a BMW', with me as a blonde posh woman in an open-top BMW driving badly also goes well, but I watch it on the monitor while Lee's make-up is being put on and decide it's too short and doesn't have enough special effects to make it interesting enough. Laughter is infectious, so a studio audience will laugh more than an audience at home.

9.10: Sketch 5 – Lee and Lance – 'Who's That Girl?' Goes down very well. Paul is very nervous about the end, when he sings 'Largo il Factotum' from Rossini's opera *The Barber of Seville*. He thinks it might look like he is being self-indulgent and showing off, and will compound his sin by singing it badly. I have to remind him all week in rehearsals that he sings it brilliantly, that he isn't showing off because I've written the sketch so he is blameless and that the audience will love it. I am right; we have to cut down the applause he gets because it goes on for a minute.

9.15: Sketch 6 – Lee and Lance – Lance's imaginary girlfriend. We thought this was the funnier sketch of the two Lee and Lances we did this week, but the audience doesn't. It still goes well enough to make the TV show, but we'll cut bits out of it that didn't get laughs.

9.25: Off for my final change into Tim Nice But Dim. The audience is getting restless now – they've been sitting in their *very* uncomfortable plastic BBC seats for nearly two and a half hours now. Rather than playing in more film, we decide to get the warm-up man to come on to try to keep them jolly, and to let those who need a pee go and have one.

9.40: Sketch 7 – Tim goes to see the bank manager. Tim gets an enormous round of applause when I come out, but it's the audience's last gasp – they're as knackered as I am. I have to go round the back to do the sketch, and although I think it's a pretty good one, it gets an end-of-the-evening reception. As soon as we finish performing it I know it's going to end up in the bin.

9.55: End. I thank the audience for coming, apologize for the length of time everything takes and go and get changed. I'm tired now, but have to keep the energy up to thank our supporting cast and to reassure the guy who played Tim's bank manager that it wasn't his fault the sketch didn't work. I blame Ian Hislop and Nick Newman, who wrote it – not because it was their fault, but because they aren't here to hear me slag them off.

10.05: DRINK! GIRLS! HOME! BED! WIFE!

END OF AUGUST–SEPTEMBER: SIX WEEKS' EDITING

This is the bit of the show I enjoy most. I'm quite a conventional person really and editing is a normal job – 9 a.m. to 6 p.m. Monday to Friday, no silly make-up, no silly voices.

The first three weeks we spend going through every single piece of film and studio material we've recorded. If everything's gone according to plan, we should have:

Film: 75 minutes
Studios: six studios of seven 3-minute sketches =
$6 \times 7 \times 3 = 126$ minutes
Total: $75 + 126 = 201$ minutes

My TV shows are 'BBC half hours', which are actually 29 minutes, to allow time for the BBC to show trailers for other shows and tell us what's on BBC2. So by the time my shows are ready for TV, they should be 29 minutes each. The title sequence and end credits take a minute together, which means that the actual sketches take up 28 minutes. A series is six programmes long, so I have to edit my 201 minutes of recorded material into $6 \times 28 = 168$ minutes for TV.

The first week editing is spent looking at the filmed stuff we've already edited, which now has the studio audience laugh track on it. We chuck away the sketches they didn't laugh at and, if we need to, we cut out parts of other sketches that didn't get the laughs we hoped for. We also cobble together sketches which are part film and part studio, like 'Wayne and Waynetta win the

Lottery', so that they become one seamless piece. (In fact, this particular sketch seemed too long when it was chopped together, so we snipped it in half and stuck it in two consecutive programmes.)

During the next two weeks we look at all the studio sketches and again chuck out the worst ones and cut down others that 'sag' in the middle. This is often quite a tricky process, as the sketches aren't designed to be cut down after filming (we hope the whole thing will be funny, so we've made no provisions for cutting in studio recording).

At the end of three weeks, all the studio and film sketches should be edited. By now we will have chucked away about twenty-five minutes of mat-erial that wasn't as good as we hoped it would be, leaving us with about 176 minutes of material, from which 168 minutes will end up on telly. This will add up to about sixty-five sketches.

In the fourth week of editing, we have to piece together the sixty-five pieces of jigsaw into six 28-minute shows. This is a nightmare. The sketches may average just under three minutes each, but some (like Julio Geordio) are only a minute, some (like Kevin losing his virginity) are more like six minutes. We start by putting pieces of paper with the names of sketches and how long they are on the floor. Then we try to work out what will go with what to make up 28 minutes, then what should go next to what (I don't like having a Gits sketch next to Self-righteous Brothers next to Modern Dad, for instance, as they're all 'elderly' characters). Also, we have to make sure we put only one sketch per character into each show. When we seem to have six shows with a good mixture of characters and length of sketches, we go back to the editor and get him to chop them together and put the titles and end sequences on each show.

At the end of the week, we look at these shows, and invariably discover that what looked good on paper on the floor doesn't look right on the screen. So we spend another couple of days chopping and changing things, until the shows all look about as good as each other. When we're finally happy with the orders of each show, they will still each be about a minute overlength, so we 'nip and tuck' little bits out here and there to get them down to time.

The last two weeks of editing are spent 'on-lining', 'grading' and 'dubbing'.

Up until now, we have edited all the programmes on Apple Mac computers. This is much quicker than editing actual film, but the quality of the picture is very poor. 'On-lining' is the process of transferring the edited computer codes back on to film.

Then the pictures are 'graded', which means making sure that the colour levels of all the different bits of film and studio material are about the same, so that the programmes don't suddenly become brighter and then darker as we move from different bits of stuff filmed under different lighting conditions.

'Dubbing' is getting the sound mix right, so that film and studio sounds the same level. It also involves changing the level of the studio audience's laughter – sometimes it's too loud and you can't hear what Paul, Kathy and I are saying, so we have to take it down. Sometimes we'll do a funny line, get a laugh, then fluff the next line, so we have to take the whole thing again. Obviously the audience don't laugh as much the second time they hear the joke as they did on take one, so in 'dubbing' we take the laugh off the first take and stick it on the pictures of the second take.

OCTOBER: FINISH

Finally, after six weeks' editing, we have six edited and dubbed tapes. We stick them on a bike and send them to the bosses at the BBC, for them to put out on TV when they like – or chuck in the bin if they don't like. At any rate, I've finally finished my bit, so it's on to the next thing – or time for a holiday!

Paul's always done a brilliant Michael Caine impression. I think Michael Caine's a brilliant actor, but no one can deny he's the same in every film he does. I had the idea of a nosy, net curtain-twitching, lonely old man and thought, 'How would Michael Caine play the part?'

MY NAME IS MICHAEL PAINE AND I AM A NOSY NEIGHBOUR

Now I've taken the liberty of placing a small device in the home of my neighbour, you know, the bloke at number twenty-seven who looks a bit like Damon Hill. Last night at seven thirty-four his old mum rang.

'Mum I'm just eating my dinner, I'll call you back,' he said. Do you know, he didn't call that woman back until nine twenty-eight. Approximately two hours later. Would Damon Hill have taken that long to return a call to his mother? I'll be honest with you. I don't know. Not a lot of people know that I don't know that, but I don't.

My name's Stanley Arbuckle, but all me pals just call me Fred

I've always liked old British films. When I was at university I used to watch a lot of them and one of my favourite things was seeing people playing cockneys who were obviously posh and unable to use the colourful language that cockneys use because swearing wasn't allowed in films. Pretend you are in a car and have just cut up a couple of cockneys in their van. The van pulls alongside you and the driver gives you a piece of his mind. Now imagine the colourful language he would say to you. This is how it would appear in an old British black and white film: 'Cor lummey, Mister! What the perishin' 'eck is you up to? Why I's a good mind to fairly give you a right flippin' duffin', so I is, Lor' luvva-duck!'

I also used to like the old propaganda films from the Second World War. The acting was often incredibly wooden. I remember one in particular called *Dawn Chorus* in which two supposedly Home Guard soldiers stood on a hilltop having a 'casual' chat about the Battle of Britain: 'Why, I reckon ol' Mister 'itler's gorn too far this time,' said one to the other, incredibly slowly and stiff as a post. 'Ay,' said the other. 'Ay,' said the first.

Bryan Elsley and I combined the propaganda and film formats for our 'Dusty and Dick' cabaret act, writing a sketch in which Bryan played a policeman and I played a delinquent youth. I threw a brick through a window and he gave me a 'clip round the lug 'ole', after which I announced in a wooden voice: 'Why, now I's a completely reformed character. I's seen the error of me ways and I's gonna shuffle orf and repay me debt to society.'

The sketch eventually appeared on TV in *Norbert Smith – A Life*, but before that I'd done a similar sketch which we filmed for my first ever appearance on *Saturday Night Live*. It was set in London, the morning after a Soviet nuclear bomb had been dropped on the city. I was the 'cockney' and John Glover, with whom I'd done *Spitting Image,* played a 'posh' fellow survivor. I surveyed the rubble that was London and said 'Corks! Old Johnny Rusky's perishin' flattened the place out a bit, ain't he?' in my best chirpy-cockney-makes-the-best-of-a-bad-situation voice. It was while filming this sketch that John Glover came up with Mr Chomondley-Warner. I'd just called him 'Posh Bloke' in the script, but had put in a silly line for myself which went, 'My name's Stanley Arbuckle, but all me pals just call me Fred,' to which John was supposed to reply, 'Hello Fred,' and shake my hand. But on the day I said my line – 'My name's Stanley Arbuckle, but all me pals just call me Fred' – and John replied, 'My name's Mr Chomondley-Warner. All my friends just call me Mr Chomondley-Warner,' which was much funnier than what I'd written. Mr Chomondley-Warner had arrived. When I came to do my series, I asked John to play Mr Chomondley-Warner alongside my Greyson, who had originated as one of my 'lives' in *Norbert Smith*. The sketches proved successful and we went on to do the Mercury telephone campaign for several years afterwards.

There were three reasons for the success of these characters. One was the authentic old-fashioned style of wooden acting that John and I perfected. Another was Geoff Posner's directing. Before we filmed the first Chomondley-Warner sketch, Geoff and I watched a recording of an address to the nation made by Sir Stafford Cripps, the post-war Chancellor of the Exchequer, from 1947. He was incredibly ill at ease in front of the camera. The piece was filmed from two camera positions. The first was a 'wide shot' of Sir Stafford at his desk, the second a 'close up' of his face. In one sequence there was a terrible cut from wide to close up. It began with a wide shot in which Sir Stafford said, 'Our number one enemy is inflation.' But after the word 'is' the picture cut to the close up of a closed-mouthed Sir Stafford's face but

with the word 'inflation' carried over from the wide shot's soundtrack. It looked incredibly silly and made Geoff and me chuckle. Over the next few years of Mr Chomondley-Warner sketches, Geoff used this style of mistake to build in hundreds of 'bad edits'. These were without a doubt the making of the Mercury commercials. The trouble with comedy adverts is that they are usually funny the first couple of times you see them, but often become irritating after that, as you know the joke that's coming up. The trick is to put in physical things that you can watch again and again without them losing their comedy impact. Geoff's 'bad

cuts' were just such devices, and kept the ads fresh however many times you saw them.

The third important thing about the Mr Chomondley-Warner sketches is the subjects we tackled. The secret was, rather than just doing old-fashioned things in an old-fashioned way, to tackle modern subjects in an old-fashioned way. So our take on the *Joy of Sex* videos was 'Mr Chomondley-Warner's Guide to Conjugal Rights'. Making love became 'bedroom unpleasantness', etc. Similarly, there are many modern programmes giving women advice, made by women, for women and with a feminist bent. We tackled

My name's Mr Chomondley-Warner. All my friends just call me Mr Chomondley-Warner

this type of thing in a thirties style with 'Women! Know Your Limits!' – helpful advice to women made by men (of course) and with a somewhat different message to its modern equivalent. Mr Chomondley-Warner works because he describes modern cultural problems from a 1930s perspective.

The Mercury commercials were written by the advertising agency rather than us, but they had to have my approval for their scripts. The first people who wrote them were brilliant and completely understood the idea of the characters. But unfortunately the ads got lots of awards and those people got promoted. Two new young boys, with little talent but lots of attitude, now came in to write them and my face dropped when I saw their efforts. There was one with me as Mr Greyson rapping along to a ghetto-blaster with a Rastafarian. 'We're trying to move your characters along,' said the talentless boys. Advertisers are always taking things that work and ruining them by 'moving them along'. What this means is that they are too stupid to see *why* something is funny and don't realize that by, say, putting Greyson rapping with a Rastafarian, they are taking him out of his time, he then becomes confusing, not funny. I was pretty brutal to the little boys, 'You're not moving the characters along, you're ruining them.' Luckily the original writers were called back in after their replacements wrote one dreadful script after another, and that bunch of ads was saved, but next year we were given more hopeless writers and the campaign ceased to be fun.

WOMEN! KNOW YOUR LIMITS!

An ordinary dinner party. Three couples. One of the men is talking. The women are laughing.

Voice Over
An ordinary dinner party. The sort of occasion we all enjoy. The men are exchanging witty stories, and look at the women, aren't they pretty – look at the way they laugh, they're delightful. But now the conversation turns to more serious matters ...

Man 1
I wonder if the Government should return to the Gold Standard.

Man 2
I think it should.

(Man 3 nods sagely.)

Man 1
Then we're all agreed.

Voice Over

But, oh dear! What's this? One of the women is about to embarrass us all ...

Woman

I think we should stay off the Gold Standard, so that the pound can reach a level that will keep our exports competitive.

(The men look at her with utter contempt.)

Voice Over

The lady has foolishly attempted to join the conversation with a wild and dangerous opinion of her own. What half-baked drivel. See how the men look at her with utter contempt.

(Man 2 gets up abruptly.)

Man 2

Daphne! We're going home.

(Woman, shamed, follows him out. Caption over this:)

'Women! Know your limits!'

Voice Over

Women! Know your limits!

(Cut to a diagram of a man and a woman's head.)

Voice Over

Look at the effect of education on a man and a woman's mind.

(Arrow of education being fed into man's head. We see his brain filling up evenly.)

Voice Over

Education passes into the mind

of a man. See how the information is evenly and tidily stored ... Now see the same thing on a woman.

(Arrow is fed into woman's head. We see her brain filling up evenly at first.)

Voice over
At first we see the same even process, but now look! Still at a reasonably low level of education her brain suddenly overloads.

(See brain becoming a frantic messy scrawl of black.)

Voice Over
She cannot take in complicated information, she becomes frantically and absurdly deranged. Too much education addles a women's mind.

(Cut to group of haggard women in white 'nut house' smocks, stooped and hairy.)

Voice Over
Look at these venomous harridans. They went to university. Hard to believe they're all under twenty-five. Yes, over-education leads to ugliness, premature ageing and beard growth.

(Cut back to dinner party as at beginning. We hear voice over.)

Voice Over
Now let's see the proper way.

Man 1
So we're all agreed, we should return to the Gold Standard.

(The men nod sagely.)

Voice Over
See how the woman restricts herself to appropriate subjects, such as kittens, dahlias, or the eccentricities of her aunt.

Woman
Why I'm sure I don't know anything about the Gold Standard, but I thought we'd give one of our sweet little kittens and some dahlias to my eccentric aunt.

Man 2
What a lovely thought, you dear, fragile, little thing. How I adore you.

(They look soppily at each other.)

Voice Over
WHAT A PLEASANT END TO A PLEASANT SCENARIO. But it's not just your thinking that should be plain and simple. It's also your attire. Watch and learn ...

(We see a woman in a vulgar forties dress outside a theatre. Her husband approaches.)

Woman
Ah, there you are, darling, shall we go in?

Man
I didn't recognize you there.

Woman
Oh, that'll be because of my new dress. I spent the entire month's housekeeping on it. Do you like it?

Man
You're a cheap-looking tart and I have nothing but loathing for your every sinew. I shall go the theatre alone.

(He storms off. A toothless foreign type approaches.)

Toothless Foreign Type
But I find you uncommon beautiful.

Voice Over
Attractive only to toothless foreign types.

(Cut to sweet picture of plainly dressed woman in some kind of chocolate box setting.)

Voice Over
Women, know your limits. In thought and dress be plain and simple, and let your natural sweetness shine through.

What's It Like

People often ask me what it's like being famous. The answer for me is that it's nicer than not being famous. One is always reading about the pressures of fame, how it turns people to drink, drugs or whatever. It's understandable that suddenly becoming the centre of attention can change you. Everyone wants to know what you think about this issue or that issue, and if you start thinking, 'Crikey, I really am frightfully important,' then when your fame subsides, as it surely will, you get a bit of a shock when you realize that people didn't care about you the person, only you the pop star, you the comic, you the 'product'. Or if you snort your pay cheques up your nose, you will go mad, as surely as night follows day, and you will find your personal life will become lonely and disruptive. I say these things because I've seen them happen to many others, but not thankfully to myself.

Fame distorts my outlook. For instance, I often go into shops where gorgeous young women assistants blush on seeing me and allow me to flirt outrageously with them. This makes me think I'm devastatingly attractive. But when I'm abroad and try to flirt with foreign shop assistants, who don't know me from Adam, their scowls of revulsion remind me that I'm fat, balding and thirty-six.

Although I'd been on telly for a couple of years doing Stavros, I first got really famous in 1988 with the success and tabloid exposure that Loadsamoney brought. But it didn't really make my head swell, as Loadsamoney didn't feel anything like as important as *Spitting Image* had been to me when I joined its voice team three years before. *Spitting Image* got 13 million viewers and *Friday Night Live* only 3 million – so as far as I was concerned I was part of a more famous team in 1985 than in 1988 with Loads. I'd had all the excitement of being part of the most successful comedy show since *Not The Nine O'Clock News* without having to be recognized. The success of Loads felt like nothing in comparison, and anyway it wasn't *me* who was famous, it was 'Loads' – the character I hid behind.

Fame affects different comedians in different ways. Some comics don't appear to get approached that much on the street. People tend to be more 'awestruck' by the likes of Rik Mayall, Rowan Atkinson and Jennifer Saunders, whereas for some reason the likes of Lenny Henry are seen as 'friendly faces' – everyone goes up to him to shake his hand and chat. I get the same as Lenny. I was brought up in a village where I knew everyone; now I pretend London, where I live, is a friendly village where I know everyone but can't remember their names. So when strangers say, 'Hi, Harry!' I go, 'Morning,' as if I knew them.

One of the worst types to be recognized in the street by are the groups of 'Kevin and Perrys' – stupid teenagers who follow me and yell, 'Harry Enfield!' when I'm a safe distance away. If I turn round and say, 'Yes! What can I do for you?' they stare at the ground and pretend to ignore me.

I did go to the opening night of *Four Weddings and a Funeral* and gawped at Liz Hurley from a yard away. So fame is great!

Being Famous?

Then I carry on and they yell my name again. It's like Grandmother's footsteps. They are really stupid!

But the most annoying people of all are the aggressive 'friendly types'. I go for a quiet drink with a book to read and get some 'Oi! NO!' type at the bar: 'Oi, Harry, cheer up it might never happen. Let me buy you a drink! CAAMON! WHAT'S THE MATTER WITH YOU? SOMETHING WRONG WITH ME, IS THERE? I SAID I'D BUY YOU A DRINK! OI! ENFIELD! YOU THINK YOU'RE TOO SMART TO HAVE A DRINK WITH ME, DO YOU? C'MERE AND DRINK THIS PINT OR I'LL GIVE YOU A SLAP!!'

On the whole, though, for me, fame has been fun. I don't go to many glitzy parties, but I did go to the opening night of *Four Weddings and a Funeral* and gawped at Liz Hurley from a yard away. So fame is great!

The Old

On every street in England there's some moany old git who's not got a good word to say about anything or anyone, but our particular Gits were based on a bloke Paul used to share an office with at Hackney council. There were three of them sharing the office: Paul, another young guy and an old git. The two younger ones would chat about sport or politics and the old git would watch contemptuously, then shake his head in disgust at what he heard, look down at his work and mumble his summary of the others' conversation in a single horrible sentence. Thus Paul and his mate would argue for a few minutes about whether Spurs or Arsenal were better and Git would listen until they'd finished and then say, 'What they wanna do is get all the players from both teams, line 'em up against a wall and shoot 'em.' Git didn't like sport much, but was something of an expert on religion: 'That Jesus geezer – he done a lot of good work for charity.' He also fancied his opinions on post-independence India: 'That Gandhi geezer – he done a lot of good work for peace. Let 'imself down wearin' flippin' nappies, though ...' Paul used to come down the pub in the evening and recount Git's words of wisdom, using the voice he uses for his 'Old Git', which I blatantly copy. When we started doing them on telly, they were mean and nasty: 'Life begins at forty! Try tellin' that to John Lennon.' But Paul and I both like to be naughty rather than nasty, and now I think they're more fun, in a horrible way.

Life begins at forty!
Try tellin' that to John Lennon

Gits

The Old Gits:
Four Funerals and a Wedding

Scene 1:

Int. Church. Day.
The Gits, dressed in Hawaiian shirts, with party poppers, etc., and ghetto-blaster playing 'Hot Hot Hot'. They are singing along.
Cut wide to reveal they are in the middle of a church funeral service. Everyone surrounding them in black.

Vicar
Excuse me, this is a funeral service.

Alf Git
We know

Fred Git
Why do you think we're celebrating?

(Someone leans over and angrily turns ghetto-blaster off and takes it from them.)

Alf Git
Yer miserable bugger. Anyone would think this was a wedding!

Fred Git
Yeah, he was our friend.

Alf Git
No he wasn't.

Fred Git
Well no, but we knew him anyway.

Alf Git
It was your fault he died.

Fred Git
What, just 'cos I left the gas running. It was you who gave him the cigar and told him to light it after we'd gone!

Alf Git
Mmmer ... It was a big explosion.

Fred Git
A very, very, very big explosion.

Alf Git
Poor old Jack.

(Cut to five pallbearers, each with a small coffin.)

Both
Rest in pieces.

(They snigger. An old woman in the pew in front turns round. Alf Git sees her.)

Alf Git
What do you want? You old ... Ivy?

Ivy
Alf? Alf ... My Alf?

Alf Git
Hello, Ivy.

Ivy
You haven't lost your looks.

(Alf sneers a coy toothy grin. The old woman smiles. Romantic music and soft focus for a couple of seconds. Cut to Alf Git shaking his head to get a grip on himself.)

Fred Git
Who's that bitch?

Alf Git
Just someone I used to know.

Fred Git
Well it's a pity she didn't die in middle age – 'cos she makes a truly revolting old woman.

Alf Git
(Hesitant) Yeah ...

Scene 2:

Ext. Entrance to the graveyard. Day. The widow and her family stand as people come past and whisper words of condolence. She thanks them. The Gits wake up. Alf Git squeezes her hand and mumbles something. She bursts into tears. The Gits walk away chuckling.

Scene 3:

Int. Living room. Day. The Wake. Alf Git looking around distracted.

Fred Git
What do you keep looking around for?

Alf Git
I can't see that Ivy.

Fred Git
That's 'cos she's not here, that's why.

Alf Git
Oh, I thought she would have come on to this.

Fred Git
Why the sudden interest in her, anyway?

Alf Git
No reason.

(Someone attempts to take a cake from the full plate Fred is holding.)

Fred Git
Leave, Bitch! *(To Alf)* Mmmer – let's go and pay our condolences to the nearest and dearest.

(We see them go over to a sofa but we don't see who is on it.)

Alf Git
You loved old Jack, didn't you? And now he's gone ...

Fred Git
All you got left is a life of misery, alone and in despair, heartbroken ...

Alf Git
No more lovely evenings by the fireside ...

Fred Git
You know what often happens in these situations, don't you?

Alf Git
One partner dies – the other one loses their will to live, and pines away ...

(Cut to sad dog on sofa.)

Voice Over Alf and Fred
Pines away ... Pines away ... Until ...

Scene 4:

Ext. Churchyard. Day. Bells ringing. Crowd round graveside.

Vicar
Ashes to ashes, dust to dust. Fido's dead, in God we trust.

(We see headstone: 'Fido – pined away 11.10.1994'. People start to walk away from the graveside. Someone grabs Alf's arm. It is Ivy.)

Ivy
Hello, Alf.

Alf Git
Ivy!

Fred Git
Not you again!

Alf Git
You weren't at Jack's wake, the other day?

Ivy
I couldn't take it, seeing you after all these years.

Alf Git
Fifty-five years, eh? He he he ... I remember you, you were a little terror you were.

Ivy
He he, yeah. Do you know what they used to call me at school? Poison Ivy.

Fred Git
Poison Ivy! That's what they should have done to you, not called you.

Ivy
I've still got the ring.

Alf Git
Our engagement ring – the one I gave you before I went off to fight Hitler's fascist hordes.

Fred Git
We never fought anyone in the war – we hid!

Alf Git
Shuddup!

(Ivy shows him the ring.)

Ivy
Is it still valid?

Alf Git
It might be my Ivy, it might just be.

Fred Git
Alf! Alf! Alf! Come on! Let's go and frighten some kiddies, eh?!

(Alf and Ivy hand in hand staring into each other's eyes as they walk away, and making baby noises. They ignore Fred, who is bleating desperately in the background. He has grabbed a cat.)

Fred Git
Alf! Look! Alf! Let's bury it alive! Ay? Alf! Alf! Alf!

Scene 5:

Int. Bedroom. Close up of Ivy's face as she moans 'Alf'. We see Alf is on top of her. Cut to close up of Alf's face as he shags her. Horrible.

Ivy
Alf! Alf! Alf!

Alf
Yes! Yes! Yes!

(Outside room, Fred is observing through crack in door.)

Fred Git
No! No! No!

Scene 6:

Later. Fred comes into the living room, where Alf and Ivy are being cuddly-wuddly. Alf is all neat and tidy. Besuited.

Alf
One step, two step, tickle you under there!

Fred Git
Oh God! What do you look like?!

Ivy
Hello, dinky doos.

Alf Git
Hello, piddly pongo.

(Fred sniffs the air in disgust.)

Fred Git
There's a terrible stink in here! And it's coming from you!

(He sniffs over Alf.)

Fred Git
I remember that smell! It's soap! What have you done to yourself, man?

Alf Git
Fred, Ivy and I are going to tie the knot.

Fred Git
Good! Make sure it's round her neck!

Ivy
Fred, we're getting married, aren't you happy for us?

Fred Git
No ... no ... no.

(He mopes sadly out of the room. Alf and Ivy cuddle up on the sofa and play 'This Little Piggy Went to Market' with Ivy's toes.)

Scene 7:

Fred Git's bedroom. Fred blubbing and rocking on his bed.

Scene 8:

Church funeral for Fred. Alf and Ivy are standing over an open coffin.

Ivy
Poor Fred, he died of a broken heart.

Alf Git
Yeah, typical Fred, he just couldn't bear me finding happiness at last. Still, look, at least he's taking it with him.

(Cut away to corpse of Fred clutching handfuls of money.)

Alf Git
I'd like to take this opportunity to read a poem, from W. H. Smith, limerick department:
There was an old Git called Fred,
Of whom I would like it said,
He's a sad loss to me,

But I've got his colostomy,
To remember him by now he's dead.

(Alf gets a container marked 'Maggots' and empties it into the open coffin.)

Alf Git
Here you are, my beauties! Have a head start on the ones in the ground!

Scene 9:

Ext. Church. Day. Alf and Ivy are married. We see them getting into their car. The car starts up and we see it start to drive off. Lots of false teeth and zimmer frames are tied to the back of it.

Ivy
We should have done this fifty years ago.

Alf Git
I know, chicken, but we've still got a good ten years in us yet, haven't we?

(Ghost of Fred springs up in the back of the car. He has a white suit on. He has brake cable and pliers.)

Fred Git
That's what you think!

(Alf applies the brakes to no

avail. *Alf and Ivy scream. We see the car crash and burst into flames.*)

Scene 10:

Cut to funeral. Mourners, including Ivy in plaster and on crutches, moving away from the graveside. Reveal gravestones of both Gits. Their ghosts are sitting on top of them in white suits.

Alf Git
Yer bugger.

Fred Git
I was only paying you back for what you done to me.

Alf Git
'Ere, I'll do a deal with you.

You dance on my grave if I can dance on yours.

Fred Git
Done!

(*They get up and start dancing on each other's graves, and singing 'Yer dead, yer bugger ...', etc. Then 'Feeling Hot Hot Hot!'...*)

Mr Don't Wanna Do It Like That

One of the classic stereotypes of British humour is the interfering mother-in-law. I had the idea of doing the 'alternative' mother-in-law, i.e. the father-in-law – the man who comes round and tells his son-in-law that he's doing his DIY wrong, mending the car wrong, the man who's always interfering in his daughter's home and has a permanent attitude of 'I've got lots more experience of life than you and I know best'. I'm hopeless at thinking up names for my characters, but I knew I had a catch phrase for him: 'You don't wanna do it like that!' – so he simply became Mr Don't Wanna Do It Like That, or Mr Don't for short. It wasn't until I was trying out clothes for him to wear that I came up with his other catch phrase. My costume designer suggested a combination of light blue and yellow, and I'd put on a golf jumper, cravat, jacket and trousers, but he still didn't feel right – I didn't know how he was going to act or sound. So the designer went off and came back with this vile flat cap and some gold-rimmed glasses. I put them on, looked in the mirror and saw this horrendous person looking at me with a look of 'Aren't I a wonderful person!' written all over his face. 'Good news! *I'm* here!' he said in an awful twangy voice. I carried on looking at the mirror, trying out phrases in my new voice. 'Hey ho! Good morningo! It's only little old me! Come to sort out your life for you!' After a few minutes I'd cut this down to 'Only ME!!!'. It seemed to say it all – the last person you wanted turning up on your doorstep was the man who said, 'Only ME!!! You don't wanna do it like that!'

After the first series we rather forgot the father-in-law angle and took him out and about to cause frustration and anger in the world at large. My favourite sketch was the hapless man in the café, who has done nothing wrong that Mr Don't can tell him he shouldn't have done. But Mr Don't has a go at him anyway ...

Mr Don't is probably the most irritating character I've ever created. I did an advert as him for Skol lager. It was ten seconds long and when we

filmed it the director told me that once the cameraman had turned the camera on, I should just do the line again and again until he told me to stop. I had to come on with my can of Skol and say, 'You don't wanna drink Skol!' then take a sip, smile to show it tasted nice and say, 'I didn't wanna say, "You don't wanna drink Skol!" You don't wanna listen to me saying, "You don't wanna drink Skol!"' The camera rolled and I came on and did the line ten times on the trot before the director said 'cut'. Then he told me to do the same again, but each time a little more quickly. When he asked for the camera to be turned on again the cameraman said to his boss, 'I'm terribly sorry, but would you mind awfully operating the camera yourself and letting me go outside for this next lot? He's so irritating I think I might punch him half-way through the take otherwise!' He was allowed to go outside, apologizing profusely to me, and never returned!

But the cameraman wasn't the only person to be irritated by Mr Don't – I'd invented him and I was punished severely for my crime. For at least two years no day would pass without at least five people yelling, 'You don't wanna do it like that!' at me. Of course, all of them thought they were the first people to say it to me ever, and knowing they meant well, I felt compelled to laugh politely each time. It was, however, extremely irritating. I only snapped once. I was in Cornwall, and had been on the beach walking the dog, which had run off and wouldn't come back. I'd spent half an hour looking for her, which had made me late for the person I was meeting in the pub for lunch. I'd already had someone saying, 'You don't wanna shout for your dog like that!' someone else saying, 'You don't wanna be in Cornwall' and someone who I asked if they'd seen a black dog replying, 'You don't wanna lose a black dog!' and I'd chortled politely to all three. Then, as I walked up a road to a different part of the beach, I passed a man with his wife and children unpacking their Renault Espace. 'You don't wanna go to *that* beach,' he shouted cheerily. That was it, I turned on my heel and pointed at him: 'YOU DON'T WANNA BE THE ONE THOUSANDTH UNORIGINAL PERSON TO SAY THAT TO ME SO FAR TODAY!!' I snapped. The poor chap's face crumpled. 'Oh!' he said. He was totally mortified, his wife was embarrassed and his children shocked. He obviously really liked my show, and I'd shouted at him in front of his family. I stomped off, but felt really sorry for the poor chap. I still feel guilty about him now.

For at least two years no day
would pass without at least five
people yelling, 'You don't wanna
do it like that!'

Lee and

Stop moaning you sad git – you have to suffer for your art

Lee and Lance are about the most conventional characters we do. They use the standard format of Thick Bloke (Lee) and Thicker Bloke (Lance). Thick Bloke thinks he's cleverer than Thicker Bloke and that everything he says is wise. Thicker Bloke's job is to say even stupider things than Thick Bloke. It's exactly the same format that Peter Cook and Dudley Moore used with Pete and Dud, only not as funny. Mel Smith and Griff Rhys Jones also use the format with their 'Head to Head' sketches.

Lance was created a couple of years before Lee, when I was doing Loadsamoney and wanted a thick mate to be the butt of my jokes. He first appeared in the video of my Loadsamoney single, 'Doin' Up The House'. When we were filming the video, I had an idea to throw my arms out sideways, with a bunch of twenty-pound notes in each hand, and accidentally hit Lance in the gob with my right fist. Because Paul wasn't an actor at the time, I thought if I told him in advance that I was going to pretend to clout him, he might do a bad 'fake' of being hit. So I didn't tell him, and when the camera rolled, I smacked him in the gob for real, cutting his lip and causing him a great deal of pain for the rest of the day. He's never let me forget this – but it looked good on the video and, as I said to him at the time, 'Stop moaning you sad git – you have to suffer for your art.' When we went on tour later in the year, Lance once again appeared, as Loads' slave. Right at the start of my set, Lance, in full harness, would drag me on stage in a golden chariot to the sound of *Carmina Burana*. As soon as the music stopped, I'd tell him to shove off and Paul'd go down the pub while I did my set. That job as Lance gave him the easiest money he's ever earnt.

When it came to doing my first series, I wanted Paul to do Lance again, because I liked him. I couldn't do Loads because I'd killed him off, so I gave him his new pal, Lee. Lee and Lance started off as car mechanics, then had a flower stall, then became decorators, then butchers, and finally, blokes with a fish stall.

Lance

Lee and Lance:

Lance
(Sings tunelessly) Who's that girl running around with you?

Lee
No, Lance, it's *(Sings perfectly)* Who's that girl running around with you?

Lance
(Sings tunelessly) Who's that girl running around with you?

Lee
No, Lance, *(Sings perfectly)* Who's that girl running around with you?

Lance
(Tunelessly) Who's that ...

Lee
No. *(Sings perfectly)* Who's!

Lance
(Tunelessly) Who's!

Lee
(Sings perfectly) Who's! *(Mimes piano key)* Bong! Bong! Bong! Who's!

Lance
Bong! Bong! Bong! *(Tunelessly)* Who's!

Lee
Bong! Bong! Bong! Who's!

Bong! Bong! Who's!

Lance
Bong! Bong! Bong! *(In tune)* Who's!

Lee
Good! Bong! Bong! Bong! That!

(Lee gets Lance's finger and moves it along the counter from the wrong note to the right one.)

Lee
(Out of tune) Bong! Bong! *(Moves up to in tune)* Bong! Bong! Bong! That!

Lance
(In tune) Bong! Bong! That!

Lee
Good Lance! Very Good! Bong! Bong! Bong! Gir-hur-hurl!

Lance
(In tune) Bong! Bong! Bong! Gir-hur-hurl!

Lee
Excellent! Running around with you!

Lance
Runn- *(Tuneless)* -ing around.

Lee
Ing! Ding! Ding! Ding!

Lance
(In tune) Running. Ding! Ding! Ding! Around with *(Tuneless)* you!

Lee
You-hoo! Ding! Dong! You-hoo!

Lance
(In tune) Runn-ing. Ding! Ding! Ding! Around with you-hoo! Ding! Dong! You-hoo!

Lee
Excellent! Now put it all together.

Lance
(In tune) Bong! Bong! Who's! Bong! Bong! That! Bong! Bong! Bong! Gir-hur-hurl! Runn-ing! Ding! Ding! Ding! Around with you-hoo! Ding! Dong! You-hoo!

Lee
Right, now do it without the bings, bongs, dings and dongs: Who's that girl running around with you?

Lance
(Sings tunelessly as at start) Who's that girl running around with you?

Who's That Girl?

Lee
No, you're right Lance, you *are* tone deaf.

Lance
See, told you! Only in English, though, I can sing in Italian alright. *(Sings fantastic short piece of opera)*

Lee
Lance, you really are weird, you know.

Lance
How do you mean?

Lee
You're just a weirdo!

Lance
I ain't gonna put up with this. I'm goin' home.

(Exits. Lee shakes head.)

Wulp! He landed her one silly mid-face on and down she went, backwards, thump went her head on the ground, and out came the inevitable volcanic scream

I got the idea for Harry and Lulu from watching friends of mine's children. A couple of years ago we were sitting in my friends' garden having lunch. Their three-year-old boy was sitting with his eleven-month-old sister on the grass. He was smiling angelically and she was wide-eyed and nodding about, the way little people of her age do. As we adults chatted away over lunch, I happened to turn to the children just at the moment when the little boy thought all grown-up eyes were off him. His clenched fist was already hurtling towards his unsuspecting sister's face – it was too late for his daft brain to make the connection between seeing my eyes were on him and telling his fist to halt in mid-air. Wulp! He landed her one silly mid-face on and down she went, backwards, thump went her head on ground and out came the inevitable volcanic scream. The little boy knew full well I'd caught him red-handed, but thought I was as stupid as him and that he could now con me with his best winning smile and the words 'Poor Jessie! She fell over!'. Sorry mate, I wasn't buying it. I duly gave evidence to the parental court and the little chap was solemnly hauled over the coals, giving us an accompanying temper tantrum and myself a furious stare of betrayal. Sibling rivalry is a terrible thing. I've a sister eighteen months older than me, who greeted the arrival of her happy little fat brother by ignoring me totally – I'd be lying on the floor wiggling my arms and legs and she would walk over me as if I were a piece of carpet.

The Toddlers

The Toddlers: Yoghurt

Dinner table. Harry on chair, Lulu in high chair, with lots of food around her mouth. Harry is finishing his yoghurt. He holds out his empty carton.

Harry
Can I have another one?

Mum
No, one's enough.

(Harry gives Mum a filthy look.)

Mum
Can you help Lulu open hers while I go to the loo?

(Harry starts to do this.)

Voice of Mum
Good boy.

(Sound of Mum exiting. Harry says to Lulu:)

Harry
Can I have it?

(She clenches yoghurt away from him.)

Lulu
Ne!

Harry
Please Lulu!

Lulu
Ne!

Harry
Oh please ... please!

(Harry pleads, Lulu is defiant. Harry starts to sob while looking longingly at yoghurt. Lulu's expression changes, she looks sad, then a bit tearful, then thrusts her yoghurt at Harry. Harry grabs it and starts to eat quickly. Lulu watches, holds out her hand, wanting it back. Without looking at her, Harry fists her in the face. She falls back and screams.)

There was a boy I was at school with called Parkins. When we arrived at school in the morning, everyone would be milling about the form room except for Parkins, who would always sit at his desk writing with his right hand and using his left arm to shield his work from our eyes, least we should want to cheat by copying his stuff (which we didn't want to – Parkins wasn't very clever). We used to take great pleasure in saying, 'Morning Parkins! How are you today?' at which he would look up from his working huddle, give us a contemptuous stare and say in his best 'Tory Boy' voice: 'None the better for your asking!'

I've always wanted to do a character based on poor, unpopular, Parkins. He seemed quite happy in his isolation, clearly finding his school friends beneath his contempt. During one of my writing sessions with Paul, we started discussing young master 'None the better for your asking!' Parkins. We started to work out what a character like him would be like: Unpopular boy – smug, friendless and supremely confident. Whatever the current youth trend was, he would be oblivious to it.

We then started talking about the young William Hague. I'm the same age as William, and when I was fifteen, I and my friends were all punks. We loved the Clash, the Sex Pistols and ATV. We thought anyone our age who wasn't a punk was old-fashioned, thick and sad. We hated the government, which was Labour at the time but we hated the Tories even more. When William Hague got up and made his famous 'Let us woll back the fwontiers of thothalithm' speech at the 1978 Tory Party conference, he naturally became our *bête noir*. Not only was he a Tory, and a goody-goody – but he was *our age*! How sad could you get!

We decided to combine Unpopular Boy with the fifteen-year-old William and got Tory Boy, an acne-faced, precocious thirteen-year-old who, unlike normal thirteen-year-olds, has no interest in girls or Oasis; his only devotion is to the Tory cause. His inspiration came not only from Parkins and William Hague, but also from the more recent offerings of Portillo, Lilley, Mawhinney, Howard and Redwood, who are Tory Boys who have never grown up. Tory Boy is in my opinion the most loathsome character I've done to date, but somehow I still feel sorry for him, with his acne and lack of friends. Of course William Hague has grown up since his Tory Boy days, and is apparently quite a nice bloke now, but I'm afraid this is unlikely to happen to Tory Boy, who will probably go bald in my next series, but be as obnoxious as ever.

He might get a friend, though. I'm afraid that before being a punk I spent my first teenage years obsessed with politics. I decided I was a communist, and my best friend Joe and I used to argue the finer points of Trotskyism versus pure Marxism when we should have been discussing girls and Slade. If I'd known Tory Boy at the time, I'm sure I would have got on well with him and had hours of happy arguments over socialism versus capitalism. So I'm currently working on a friend for Tory Boy based on a thirteen-year-old nerd called Harry Enfield. Ginger Leftie will be a New Labour version of Tory Boy, and they'll be best pals!

Tory Boy

An acne-faced, precocious thirteen-year-old who, unlike normal thirteen-year-olds, has no interest in girls or Oasis; his only devotion is to the Tory cause

TORY BOY

Mum, Dad and Tory Boy round the breakfast table. Mum is looking at her bank statement.

Mum
Oh, the increase on my allowance has come through – thanks.

Dad
Good.

Tory Boy
Increase?

Mum
Yes, Dad's increased my allowance.

Tory Boy
An increase, Father! I haven't noticed a significant increase in her productivity!

Dad
Ah, but things go up in price, Tory Boy and she hasn't had any extra money for a couple of years.

Tory Boy
How much is this increase?

Dad
None of your business.

Tory Boy
How much is this increase?

Mum
Look, Dad's given me an extra £80 a month, if you really must know.

(Tory Boy picks up her statement, reads:)

Tory Boy
£580 – that's an increase of 16 per cent. Way above the level of inflation and totally unacceptable.

Dad
Look! Food's gone up a lot, so have the bills, plus clothes – you're a growing boy – you cost a lot more ...

Tory Boy
Then she should economize! It's no good throwing money at the problem! Her cleaning is below par, as is her cooking! These services should be put out to competitive tender! Then her functions would be performed more cheaply and efficiently with no extra cost to you, the allowance-payer ... I have your interest at heart, Father, you are the wage-earner. Where would we be without you? Marvellous!

Mum
Oi! I run this house, and I'll cook and clean as I see fit. It's a tough job being your mum, and I deserve the extra money.

Tory Boy
Mother! Nobody goes into motherhood for the money. Oh no, it's a vocation, and a very honest and valuable one. Where would we be as a nation, without our mothers? But when you start to hold the family to ransom with your unrealistic and selfish demands, your 'I'm all right Jack' mentality, then we say no! No! The line is drawn here and you don't cross it!

Dad
Tory Boy! If you carry on like this, I'll send you to your room ... Is that clear?

Tory Boy
(Sheepish) Yes.

Dad
Good. Get on with your breakfast.

(Tory Boy gets a piece of paper out of his pocket and hands it to his father.)

Tory Boy
Mother, may I eat my Cocopops next door in front of *The Frost Report*?

Mum
Go on then.

Tory Boy
Thank you. The house is adjourned!

(Exits.)

Quickies and

In my third series – *Harry Enfield and Chums,* series one – as well as the regular characters, we invented a number of short characters who appeared several times in one programme, or popped up throughout the series.

Brian Bewildered

I was in a pub about three years ago and this man of about forty-five came over and started chatting to me. He was very polite and quite earnest, wearing a permanent frown on his forehead. He also had an incredibly squeaky voice, poor chap, which seemed at odds with his serious manner. The more serious he became, the more squeaky he got and the more I wanted to giggle, but obviously couldn't. At one point he started telling me about some invasion of privacy I'd suffered at the hands of the press, and became so outraged and squeaky that I expected every dog in the neighbourhood to come rushing through the door at any moment. For weeks afterwards I couldn't stop doing this chap's voice and practising being outraged and bewildered by things I saw in the street, like people getting on a bus ('A big red thing come along and took all the people away! Just took 'em off! Bang! Gone! I mean what's going on there?'). I did him as a one-off character, and even though he was based on someone perfectly sane, he got more and more bewildered as the sketches went on, and I got a lot of complaints from mental health charities – oops! For some reason he was incredibly popular with women. Which just goes to show that birds are nutters.

Costume is very important to my characters – if I don't feel right in the costume, I can't do the character properly. Brian Bewildered is a good illustration of this. We filmed all the sketches in one afternoon and I was incredibly unhappy about my performance. For some reason he just wasn't funny. The camera crew didn't laugh. Nobody did. At the end of the day, I was prepared to chuck everything we'd shot in the bin. I was discussing my frustration with my costume designer and she told me she thought the gloves were wrong. I'd had the idea of giving Brian gloves joined together by a long piece of elastic going through my anorak, like I had as a child to prevent me losing them. When we filmed I had bare hands with gloves flapping at my wrists. So I took them off and tried the character out in the wardrobe mirror. He felt much better. For some reason I was now confident enough to make Brian funny. We filmed all the sketches again two days later without gloves and this time the camera crew were roaring with laughter. Before, he'd felt wrong. Now he felt right. That made all the difference.

One-offs

Dr Philip Boyish-Good-Looks
A TV doctor on programmes like *Richard and Judy* and *GMTV*. Dr Philip was Paul's idea – the doctor who all the old dears are in love with, but not as much as he's in love with himself. Very clean and very creepy, Dr Philip lives alone with his collection of teddy bears – yuk!

The Aliens
'English for Aliens' is one of my favourite sketches, but they only appeared once, because the make-up took five hours and was incredibly hot and uncomfortable, and despite Paul and Charlie's pleas I refused to do them again. The day after the sketch went out, I was walking down a street in London when this lorry screeched to a halt just past me. The driver got out and, without looking at me at all, ran up to a plane tree that was growing by the pavement, pointed at it and squeaked, 'Tree!' He then ran back to his lorry and drove off. A couple of tourists watched this display open-mouthed. Only the British. It cheered me up for the rest of the day.

Modern Dad
Poor old Modern Dad was Richard Preddy and Gary Howe's idea. It appealed to me because I've lots of gay friends who've been through similar experiences. Few parents over sixty understand the 'progressive' comings and goings of their children, but they love them, so they try their best. I based my character on my father, who is from a much more traditional generation, and always tried just-that-little-bit-too-hard with my girlfriends, knowing that, in the modern world, he mustn't voice his old-fashioned disapproval of relationships outside wedlock. If you've ever seen my dad on *Watchdog,* you'll know how similar Modern Dad is to him. Modern Dad worked so well because Ben, who played my son, and his boyfriend Ewan (Spud from *Trainspotting*) were so sympathetic. They didn't 'camp it up' – they were just a normal, nice couple. You feel sorry for them, for me and for Mum. The sketch was basically 'What if a gay couple had come to stay at Fawlty Towers?'.

Camp Jockeys
The Camp Jockeys were the creations of Graham Linehan and Arthur Matthews, the writers of *Father Ted.* Like Father Ted, they are very silly. I like them.

For the Sake of the Children
I had the idea for this dreadful twosome at a time when lots of politicians were running down single-parent families, and being all smart-alec and pious about the sanctity of the traditional family. The vast majority of single-parent families are women whose foul husbands have gone off with bimbos, leaving them to bring up the children and be looked down on by the politicians. It became totally uncontroversial to say that all children were better off if they lived with both parents in a traditional family. I thought that this was wrong, and invented this couple, who clearly detest each other, but are staying together 'for the sake of the children'. This is the blackest humour I do, and many people have told me how uncomfortable the couple make them feel. It's not that I think that they should necessarily split up, I'm just trying to make the point that children who live with only one parent are often better off than those who live with two who act like babies. Relationships are never black and white, and politicians of all parties should keep their hypocritical noses out of people's private lives.

Il Postino Pat
Ian Hislop and Nick Newman's idea – how could I resist it! It was brilliant fun to make. Usually when we're filming outside, Paul and I share a caravan to dress and relax in, Kathy has her own, and all the supporting actors have to muck in together. On the day we shot 'Il Postino Pat', Kathy wasn't there, so there were only two caravans – mine and Paul's said 'Dawn French' on it,

with a massive star under her name. The other one said, 'Paul, Harry and the other supporting actors'. They'd put champagne, strawberries and flowers in our usual caravan for Dawn, instead of the usual half jar of Nescafé. The crew found it fantastically amusing, and I suppose Paul and I would have done if we'd been luvvie actors – they like that kind of joke. But we're not, we're comedians, and comedians don't like jokes unless they tell them themselves, so we kicked a few heads in and gave Ms French a good slapping.

Leslie Norris

Leslie Norris was Paul and Charlie's brilliant creation – the barman who tries his best to be 'your friendly local publican' but can't remember the names of any of his regulars, or what they drink, or what day it is, or what planet he's on. The scripts were immensely funny, but I found them terribly difficult to learn as, like Leslie, they had no internal logic. I performed Leslie four times, but of the sketches we did I was only happy with my performance in one of them. In the others I'm trying so desperately hard to remember the lines that I've a permanent look of fear in my eyes, which makes the character not very relaxed or funny. I dropped Leslie from the line-up after my Christmas special, because I wasn't very good at him. Sorry, Paul and Charlie.

The Naughty American Actor

Another mad idea from the writers of *Father Ted*.

Modern Dad

A couple in their forties or fifties, sitting in their front room. Dad is very nervous.

Mum
Look, they'll be here soon, just relax, will you, treat them the same as any other couple.

Dad
Fine, right. You're quite right.

(Doorbell rings, she answers it.)

Mum
They're just two normal people in love.

Dad
Yes, yes, you're right. Fine.

(Opens door, two young men come in.)

Mum
(Kissing the son) Hello, love.

Tom
Hi, Mum ... Dad ... this is Dominic.

Dad
Hello, Tom – yes, hello, nice to meet you – this is the first time Tom's introduced us to one of his, um, um, special friends. Yes! Lovely. So, you're dominant, then? Christ, sorry, so you're Dominic?

Dominic
I'm Dominic, yes.

Dad
Yes! Awfully nice and completely normal to meet you. *(Shakes hand vigorously)* Jolly good! *(Wipes hands on trousers)*

Dominic
Nice to meet you too.

Dad
Not too nice, I hope! *(Laughs much too boisterously)* Ha ha ha!

Mum
(Giving a glass of wine to everyone) There we go.

Dominic
Thanks.

Mum
(To Dad) Nice relaxing drink.

Dad
Excellent! Ah well, everyone! Bottoms up – I'm so sorry! I didn't mean to, sorry, I mean 'Queers!' CHEERS! CHEERS EVERYONE! CHEERS! *(Clinks glasses over-enthusiastically)* JOLLY GOOD!

Mum
Dinner's nearly ready. Barry, will you come and carve!

Dad
Yup! Sure! OK! That's a manly job *(Backing out of room to kitchen)* You two sit down and make yourselves at homo – HOME! HOME! HOME!

(Cut to meal in swing.)

Tom
... I think we'll probably head back for London about nine.

Mum
Are you sure, darling? You're both welcome to stay the night if you want.

(Dad looks shocked.)

Tom
Thanks, Mum, but we've got to get back.

Dad
Phew! ... This chicken's lovely! Mmm!

Tom
We've got to got to a funeral tomorrow, a friend of Dominic's died the week before last.

Mum
I'm so sorry.

Dad
Was he a ... good friend?

Dominic
Yes, a really close friend.

(Dad drops his knife and fork and, terrified, looks from Dominic to Tom.)

Dad
And he died ...

Tom
... in a car crash, yes.

Dad
OH, THANK GOD FOR THAT! Oh, thank the LORD! Oh dear *(Gulps at his drink)* Oh, I'm so sorry, I thought he might have died of, of ...

Tom
Of what?

Dad
Of ... *(Coughs)*

Dominic
Of what?

Dad
Of ... *(Coughs again)*

Tom
Do you mean of Aids?

Dad
Aids! Oh! I hadn't thought of that!

Tom
Dad!

Dad
So he died in a car crash then, and not of Aids?

Dominic
That's right!

Dad
You sure he didn't have Aids, but still died in a car crash?

Dominic
No, he didn't have Aids, I'm positive.

Dad
You're positive!

Dominic
Yes.

Dad
You're positive! He's positive! Mum! He's positive! Oh My God! it's alright, son! We still love you!

Tom
For Christ's sake, Dad! Dominic is positive his

friend didn't die of Aids! He is not HIV positive! Neither am I! We have both had tests and we are fine! Now will you please calm down and relax.

Dad
I'm so sorry! I really am. You'll have to forgive me, I'm not used to ...

Dominic
That's OK.

Tom
It's alright, Dad.

Dad
Thanks ... Ah well! Best get on with the grub — football's on in a bit.

Dominic
I don't really follow football.

Dad
Ha! What do you mean? What are you – a poof? – AAARGH!!

FOR THE SAKE
OF THE

Jill is on phone to friend. Throughout the conversation Tom flinches. Flinching gets worse.

Mum
No I know exactly what you mean, someone needs to tell her that she hasn't got the legs for skirts that length any more ... mmm ... mmmm ... ha ha ha! No I couldn't either, you think she'd just look in the mirror and see ... OK, look I'd better go, I've got to start cooking – I'll speak to you tomorrow, Sarah ... take care ... bye.

Dad
Uurgh, God.

Mum
What's the matter with you?

Dad
Uurgh! Nothing, sorry, don't worry about it.

Mum
No, you're sitting there through my whole phone call flinching. What is it?

Dad
Look! It's my problem, OK! I just can't bear the sound of your voice – it drives me up the wall – I'll deal with it. End of story.

Mum
Oh well, thanks a lot!

Dad
Well you asked!

Mum
What's wrong with my voice?

Dad
Huh! There is nothing inherently wrong with your voice. It is just that I don't happen to like the tone of it. If it

CHILDREN

was up here – fine. If it was down here – again, fine. But like this, this relentless irritating drone, I happen to find not particularly to my taste.

Mum
Oh I see. We've been married for fifteen years and suddenly my voice has started to irritate you ...

(Tom takes a slurp of tea.)

Mum
Uurgh!

Dad
Are you having a fit or something?

Mum
No. It's just that other people seem to be able to drink tea without making it look and sound like a pig with its snout in the trough.

Dad
Well, if it disturbs you, you are quite free to leave and go and start making your usual slap-dash job of the dinner.

(Son, fourteen, enters.)

Tom
'Lo.

Dad
Tom! Your mother and I were just discussing when the hell she was going to make the dinner.

Mum
And if your father hadn't made me feel physically sick I'd have made it by now and he'd be grunting and burping his way through it, as is his custom.

Tom
I'm going to change.

(They shout after him.)

Mum
Alright, darling, I love you.

Dad
I love you more!

(Exits.)

Mum
God you're babyish.

Dad
Of course I love him more. You are the one who wants a divorce. I am the one who insists we wait until he is old enough to leave home. I love him as much as I loath you, which is why I am keeping this family together – for his sake! ... What's the matter, have you gone deaf as well as saggy?

Mum
Sorry, I wasn't listening. I was just trying to remember the date on which you turned into the world's biggest tosser!

The Ones That

Along with the characters that have worked on my shows, there are many who haven't.

Mr Kudere
Mr Kudere was a middle-aged bloke I came up with who was always moaning – 'Cuh Dear!' being his relentless catch phrase. In rehearsal Paul thought he was crap, Kathy thought he was crap, the producer Harry Thompson thought he was crap and I thought he was great. I performed it in front of the studio audience, and they thought he was crap. So that was the end of him.

The Bores
The Bores appeared in my first series. They were basically car bores: they told bad jokes and then went UMMMM!! after the punchline to cover the lack of laughter:

Bore 1
What are we driving at the moment ?
Bore 2
Bit of a Rover 416 Gti.
Bore 1
Very reasonable motor – does she go?
Bore2
Like the wife after a glass of sherry. Ummm!
Bore 2:
Nyar! Amusing!

Unfortunately, even though we all found them funny, the audience didn't.

Bird In A BMW
This was me as Tim Nice But Dim's girlfriend, a hideous Sloane in an open-top BMW who barged into the front of a queue of cars at traffic lights while smiling and waving 'Hanks! Hanks a lot!' to the driver whose car would be smashed up if he didn't let her in, and 'Horry! Hawfully horry!' to drivers whose cars she bashed in her effort to get to the wine bar asap.

A quiet London street. Cars are parked along the side. A young Sloane woman with blonde hair and sunglasses gets into an open-top BMW. She starts the engine and whizzes out of her parking space, bashing the car in front. The driver looks startled.

Bird in BMW
Horry!

(She zooms off down the road, cuttting up the car behind her. She waves to the car.)

Bird in BMW
Horry!

(A busy main road. She comes straight out of a side road without stopping. Cars screech to a halt and hit their horns. She waves.)

Bird in BMW
Horry! Hanks! Horry!

(She barges into traffic on the other side of

Got Away

the road and zooms off. Cut to shop: 'Posh Designer Clothes'. She comes out with masses of shopping, trots to BMW parked on a zebra crossing. An irate traffic warden wags his finger at her, gives her a ticket and tells her off in no uncertain terms.)

Bird in BMW
Eugh! Horry horry horry horry horry! Byeee!

(She zooms off, etc.)

We did one sketch with her screaming around the streets bashing things up but when I saw the film at the editors, I thought it was badly shot and didn't have enough special effects, so I threw it in the bin.

Mr Dead
I love Mr Dead. He was Dave Cummings' idea, and I thought he'd appeal to people even if they didn't know the American sit-com *Mr Ed*, because I thought the idea of a hick whose best friend was a corpse was really funny anyway. But I was wrong. Only a smattering of highly intelligent people like me found Mr Dead funny!

New Sketches
Never before seen or read

These are sketches that might or might not
appear in the Christmas show.

Tim Nice But Dim Meets an Alien

The glass doors of an empty department store, on which are displayed the store's opening times, at the bottom of which are the words 'closed all day Sunday'. We reveal Tim standing patiently waiting for the store to open, reading the Sunday Telegraph. The street is deserted. A green alien with big ears etc. approaches him. Tim looks up and sees alien. He closes his paper. There is a pause while the two look at each other. Then Tim proffers a hand.

Tim
Tim Nice But Dim, how d'yer do?

(Alien takes his hand and squeezes it. Tim gets an electric zap that makes his hair stand on end. Tim gets his hand away and laughs.)

Tim
Ha ha! Excellent prank! I used to have one of those hand zappers but I lent it to Charlie and he had it confiscated by a policeman for using it on the Queen Mum – some people have no sense of humour
...

(Alien just stares at Tim. Tim gestures at shop.)

Tim

Should've opened by now! Cuh! ... what line of work are you in? Mmmm.

Alien

I have come to take over.

Tim

Right! Do you know Toby Peckenham-Filtch? He's in takeovers, bloody good business actually – but not for those with dicky tick-ers – frightfully high stress I should imagine, mmm ...

Alien

I have come to take over your planet.

Tim

Gosh! Wow! You must work for the big boys then! Toby's more into merging booksellers with chip-shop chains, that sort of thing.

Alien

Be quiet!

Tim

It is v. quiet, isn't it – that's because it's Sunday and the shops are all closed because everyone's gone to their country pads for the weekend. Where do you live?

Alien

I am from far away.

Tim

Really? Well, with house prices going crazy again one has to look further away to get anything decent. Do you know Justin and Za Za Winkworth-Stanley? They've just moved to Brondesbury.

Alien
Another planet!

Tim
Could well be, yah, the amount of time it takes to get there from Fulham. Not a bad house but a really good garden – 100-footer.

Alien
Show me your leaders.

Tim
Right … right of course … *(He opens centre of Telegraph and shows the leading articles to alien)* There's a good one on birching hunt saboteurs – makes a lot of sense – then one on birching chaps who filtch car wirelesses – bloody good idea – and one on bringing back the birch in schools – rum idea if you ask me …

Alien
I want to meet your masters!

Tim
No you don't. My masters are exactly why they don't want to bring back birching in schools. Youch! Especially Wacko Henderson. Mind you, one had to admire his skill, he could pin-stripe your bot better than a Savile Row shirtmaker.

Alien
You will be terminated!

Tim

I know, technically my contract's terminated at the end of the month, although I've been on fully paid leave since I was caught playing Tomb Raider on the desktop while my Far Eastern business crashed on the Nikkei. That Lara Croft, eh? Phwoar! Top totty!

Alien

You earthlings are too thick. Domination would be boring ...

Tim

I dunno, I've always quite fancied being dominated – especially by Lara Croft.

Alien

I return to my ship!

Tim

Do you sail? Excellent! I've got a part share in a bit of a 42-footer down at Chi' if you fancy coming along one day – I've got a pic of her in my wallet here ...

(Tim fumbles in wallet. Alien disappears into thin air. Tim looks up.)

Tim

Here! Oh, he's gone. What a thoroughly nice bloke ...

(Tim bashes on store doors.)

Tim

Hullo! Anyone at home! I need to buy some hankies!...

Raising the Titanic

Voice Over

And now on BBC1, a programme on the recent unsuccessful attempt to raise the Titanic.

(Cut to Waynetta in bed looking very fat with empty pizza boxes all around, smoking a fag.)

Wayne

Get up you lazy fat cow.

Waynetta

I am smoking a fag!

Toddlers

Close up of Lulu's face looking a bit surprised. She starts to sway vigorously, then screams. Camera pulls back to reveal her on top of Christmas tree, which Harry is shaking violently.

As I said at the beginning of this book, the way I got into the comedy business is by no means the only way – it's just my personal experience. Now's a better time than ever before to become a comedian. There are more comedy clubs to go to and try your luck at than ever before, more TV channels looking for new acts and programmes – all TV executives are desperate for good new comedy. If you don't want to be a comedian, maybe you know someone funny enough who does. It takes a bit of talent, a bit of luck, and a lot of determination. I've been booed off, yelled at, come last in talent contests, and worst of all, had my jokes greeted by the deafening silence of two hundred bored faces, but still made it in the end, and I know many others who've suffered far worse than me on the way up. But it's all been fun, and I hope it continues to be.

Harry Enfield, July 1997

Epilogue

With special thanks to:
Kathy Burke, Paul Whitehouse, Charlie Higson, Gary Bleasdale, Mark Moraghan,
Lavinia Bertram, Bill Thomas, Carla Mendonca, Sherry John, Scott Marshall, Jon Glover,
Susan Field, Brian Elsley, Julia St John, Janet Mitchell, Henrietta Branwell, E. Vaudrey,
Claire Driver, Susan Field, Lucinda Fisher, Dawn French, Geoffrey Perkins, Ian Hislop,
Nick Newman, Graham Linehan, Arthur Mathews, Richard Preddy, Gary Howe,
Hat Trick Productions, Tiger Aspect Productions, BBC, Channel 4, LWT, HHCL,
Mercury and PBJ Management.

And a very special thanks to photographers Simon Farrell, Chris Ridley and Steve Pyke.

Book design by Tony Fleetwood.